Collaborate

Tools and Techniques for Productive Meetings

John Canfield

with Greg Smith

Black Lake Press
TELL YOUR STORY
BLACKLAKEPRESS.COM

Cover design by Greg Smith of Black Lake Studio.

Published by Black Lake Press of Holland, Michigan.
Black Lake Press is a division of Black Lake Studio, LLC.
Direct inquiries to Black Lake Press at *www.blacklakepress.com*.

ISBN 978-0-9824446-9-6

*Dedicated to the thousands of my clients
who had the courage to wonder, change,
and improve their workplaces.*

Table of Contents

Introduction

Collaborate, the second part of the *Good Thinking Series,* follows *Think or Sink: A Parable of Collaboration.* The premise of the *Good Thinking Series* is that that thinking drives performance. Thinking is an improvable skill. Those of us who advocate performance improvement are constantly searching for better ways to think about things.

The operative verb in the series is "collaborate," which I define as a team's deliberate ability to build simultaneously both great decisions *and* great buy in. Decisions without support have no impact. Supporting weak decisions is not worth the effort. Effective leaders have come to know they need to lead in such a way that they can help both happen through their teams, throughout their organizations.

A common speed bump—and too often a road block to good thinking—is how one thinks about conflict.

In *Think or Sink,* Louise is a "competer" and used conflict to keep employees and others at a distance, which is a tough spot to collaborate from. Mark, an "accomodater," works hard to avoid conflict by smoothing situations to create artificial harmony. Ugh. Chuck, the collaborator, thinks of conflict as merely the point when people discover they have different perceptions, points of view, and opinions. Armed with the belief that conflict is actually synonymous with options, Chuck can help lead his team through robust dialogue and generate great decisions that the team supports.

The *Good Thinking Series* is intended to be a primer to the thinking—the mental operating system—of both good leaders and followers, who are intent on learning to do the hard work of building win-win solutions. Very short of any ten-pound comprehensive bible of collaboration, my hope is that the Good Thinking series helps you get started in learning to think, behave, and lead collaboratively—or help you to get much better at it than you now are.

Good Thinking Series Parts 2-4 will introduce specific tools that guide a team's thinking while they work to accomplish a specific task. Without the assistance of the tools, conversations are random and political—which is why so many of us dislike meetings. This second part, *Collaborate,* will help you learn to use effective communication approaches for both small and large teams.

So, why bother? While Lean and Six Sigma efforts help companies save millions of dollars by targeting and eliminating waste and defects, *The Good Thinking Series* targets dysfunctional behavior in organizations, which is the big elephant in the living room. If we can talk about how a process can be improved, we should be able to talk about how *people* can be improved. And, better yet, how people can learn to want to and be able to improve themselves, to become more effective, contributing members to the team. It may be harder to put a dollar amount on the waste and defects due to dysfunctional behavior, but as W.E. Deming would say, the dollar amount is "unknown and unknowable," and obviously deserves the effort to improve it. Redirecting, and minimizing/eliminating the dysfunctional behavior, can be like removing a large painful splinter. Hurts while it's in place, soon forgotten when it's gone.

While people may not like meetings, they are the primary social forum for work around the world. As such they're not going away. Improving how we work in meetings is the target of the Good Thinking Series. Learning to collaborate productively can be a real breath of fresh air for leaders and employees.

If you have ever fixed something with a favorite tool, you'd likely be able to describe this tool as not so pretty, a bit scratched up, but very useful. I hope you come to look at Collaborate, and the rest of the *Good Thinking Series* as such tools.

I am primarily a seminar leader and meeting facilitator. I am most interested in helping clients, and readers, to learn and use new skills. I notice that more sticks with the people in my seminars when I repeat important ideas about thinking processes. The teacher's creed is, "Tell them what you're going to tell them, tell them, and then tell them what you told them." As a result, I have repeated ideas in some sections. Hopefully, when you notice this it confirms that you now know the new approach. For those who read only selective chapters, they will then see the idea for the first time. Without the repeated idea, the single chapter would be less useful.

1
Why Collaborate?

Business Success Fundamentals from 45,000 Feet

Simply and fundamentally, the success of a business depends on what gets done by everyone–both the leaders and the employees. And nothing gets done if decisions aren't made. Decisions are the stepping-stones to action. And no matter how brilliant a decision may be, it has marginal impact when the leaders and employees don't support it.

Therefore, success depends on the number of great decisions made and supported by both leaders and employees. Companies depending on only a few decision makers and ho-hum support from their employees cannot compete over the long term. Developing, managing, improving, and leading an effective business means building both great decisions and great support. Productive collaboration does both. Collaboration can become the key business improvement strategy in your organization.

Starting Point

Employee and leadership teams do the work in organizations around the world today. Businesses realize that they need the range of ideas and the implied support that comes when a group works on a project together. These teams also include a wide variety of personalities, styles, needs, and agendas. How to get this group of people to do good work is often a challenge. One frequent mantra for an improvement strategy is to "collaborate." When a team says they will collaborate, it suggests that people are going to work together and hence make more progress.

Productive collaboration requires more than just putting people in the same room. In my experience just getting people together hasn't helped all that much. Done poorly, collaboration builds half-baked ideas, half-heartedly supported by some of the team's members. When productive collaboration isn't taking place, there is too much noise or too much quiet, too much argument or too little discussion. Too much time is invested for such poor results.

These gatherings are often described as "dysfunctional," which means that a thing is not functioning properly, or not in a way that would achieve its purpose. Consider that meetings are the primary place where business work gets done. Too many of our meetings are dysfunctional, because they don't produce great decisions with great support.

Collaboration can be so much more than just assembling as a team to do work. Collaboration done well builds decisions better than anyone expected, supported enthusiastically by all of the team's members. Opinions are substantiated by data. Goals are developed and documented by the team. The team generates, considers, selects, and implements its own decisions. There is lots of conversation, lots of wall charts, lots of productive learning. Team performance improves, and improved team morale follows quickly.

The *Good Thinking Series* of books can help you learn that you don't have to be captive to personal agendas or corporate dysfunction. We can understand why our meetings are frustrating, why our projects don't turn out like we expected, and why our goals are just beyond our grasp. We can understand why our teams seem to achieve less than the sum of the team members' abilities. We can recognize unhealthy expectations, ineffective thought patterns, and unproductive communication styles.

My strategy to improve corporate performance is based on the following observations:

Improved Company Performance
↑
Improved Decisions & Support
↑
Improved Ideas
↑
Improved Thinking

So, if I really want to improve a situation, I should be asking myself "What is the best way to think about this?"

We can do something about the way we think. We can use productive collaboration tools that guide our thinking to leverage our strengths and limit our weaknesses. We are all frustrated when we work together and don't have much to show for it. But if we think more deliberately about what we are trying to accomplish and what can sabotage those goals, we can make use of structured collaboration tools that bring a return on investment of time and energy. We can become more effective together because we begin to think more effectively and honestly about who we are, what we're trying to accomplish, and how to collaborate to achieve it.

Effective collaboration deliberately uses approaches, tools, and techniques that temporarily guide a team's thinking towards more productive ends. "Collaboration" without a guide to focus thinking is often random, unproductive, and diminished by interpersonal conflict.

Productive Collaboration Has Two Crucial Components

We will learn that the first component of effective collaboration is asking the team to identify the best alternative–to make a really good decision.

A second component is to deliberately build support for the team's selections by organizing the discussion to promote participant contribution and buy-in.

It is this combination of both better decisions and better support that provides team decisions, which generate significant business impact.

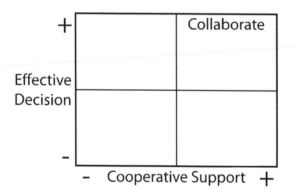

The impact of this combination cannot be overstated. Consider a situation where a leader (let's call them a "competer") makes the decision about a particular issue that affects many others. They think that decision making is their job. They then go to the team to announce the decision and ask for their support, ask for questions, and leave the group.

The group will find a water cooler and share their feelings and opinions about the decision: "Where did that come from?" "That will never work," "I'm just going to lay low until the dust settles," etc. I suggest that the leader's team, with this thinking, will be unable to support the decision to their full capacity and will generate a suboptimal result on the project.

Conversely, a second leader (let's call them an "accommodator"), spends all sorts of time with the team working hard to make sure everyone gets heard and feels good about the decision. But such a team tends to base its decisions on the members' opinions and perceptions, and usually ends up making poor decisions. Good support of a bad decision will also generate a suboptimal result on the project.

In summary, productive collaboration:

- **Is deliberate.** It does not happen accidentally or randomly.
- **Builds better options** by comparing data to listed goals.
- **Builds buy-in** by being so interactive that it allows each team member to be heard (people support what they help create).
- **Works best when the team uses effective Tools** which guide a team's thinking in a very interactive way.

Think or Sink: A Parable of Collaboration

The *Good Thinking Series'* first book, *Think or Sink: A Parable of Collaboration,* highlights three teams' performance that results from the thinking of the three leaders (Louise, Chuck, and Mark) and their teams.

In reading the first book you are encouraged to wonder how the three leaders are different, and why and how their three teams get different results. As the appendix in

Think or Sink explains, the developing results of the three leaders is painfully predictable. Leadership style does have a significant (and again, predictable) effect on team results.

If Chuck in *Think or Sink* did generate predictable results why not duplicate Chuck? I am not suggesting I only want Chucks for all leaders. I only want all my leaders to be successful. Good leaders can be wonderfully diverse. What did Chuck do differently, how did he think or behave differently? Successfully implementing collaboration skills will have lots of different looks and feels. I a strongly suggesting that successful leaders need to work on producing both good decisions and good support.

Collaborate - Book Scope

This second book in my *Good Thinking* series is for optimists, for idealistic people, people who believe they can have a positive influence on their organizations, generate better results, and have more fun in the doing. If you read *Think or Sink,* and wanted more, you are likely an optimist. Bad bosses are not inevitable. There are many good and great bosses. This book will help those who want to help their teams collaborate deliberately – to make better decisions for the team, and build better buy in from the team.

This is not intended to sound Pollyannish. This is intended to encourage those readers of *Think or Sink* to avoid working with the Louise's and Marks of the world, but more importantly, not to be the Louises and Marks of the world. This book and its approach are neither simple nor simplistic–they are fundamental. The Good Thinking Series of Think or Sink books is intended to provide you with choices in how you think and how you lead.

2
Collaboration Speed Bumps and Roadblocks

The Nature of the Beast

As *Think or Sink* illustrated, most dysfunctional work behavior is driven by person-centered thinking. We take our eye off the problem that we are working together to solve and operate based on what is best for us personally. Sometimes that is naked ambition, but often it is more subtle than that. Our preferences and opinions drive us, and while loyalty to people is an admirable trait it can often skew how we receive input from other people in meetings. We filter everything through our own wants, needs, and biases, often carelessly by default.

In other words, the problem isn't just that we "do" meetings the wrong way but that we think the wrong way about our meetings. Bad thinking almost guarantees the dysfunctional results. If we think of our meetings as irrelevant processes, unworthy of deliberate planning and techniques, the meetings are taken hostage by our passions and personalities and power plays. If we think about our meetings as arenas to advance our own needs, values, alliances, and objectives, then our meetings will never really be about solving problems. If we operate from me-centered thinking and instincts then we will fall into any one of the dysfunctional, less helpful behaviors, never emerging to collaborate and achieve authentic consensus around a solution to the problem we are meeting to solve.

What's needed is a way to change the thinking to change the behavior, a way to pull the thinking from person-driven argument to data-driven, robust dialogue. If we let our meetings be about the data and not drama, our meetings will produce better ideas, behaviors, and performance. This can include the same level of emotion and energy, but pulled from defending one's position to building a team's best option. We can plunge into our different ideas, and even provoke spirited intellectual debate for the purpose of uncovering a treasure trove of options for the group to explore. These options give us pathways to solve the problem. We can choose between conflict (chaos) and productive collaboration (alignment & synergy).

The Speed Bumps of Personal Differences

To successfully facilitate a decision making meeting I do not find it necessary or useful to differentiate or unpack the many ways people can be different to help a team collaborate. We could (some people have) fill whole books just talking about all the things that divide us. Despite all those, we still must work together to solve problems and accomplish tasks. To do that we have to have meetings, and we cannot (or should not) pick and choose who we meet with based on whether or not they will agree with us. I would rather that we appreciate our differences and provide a process that the whole team can follow to move towards achieving its mutual goals, not the agendas of the separate members.

Nevertheless, understanding the fundamental types of differences that impede or slow down our meetings has value, if only so that we can learn to minimize any negative effect of the forces at play. Three categories I find useful are personal differences, team stage differences, and change initiative differences.

Personal differences can be highlighted using tools that have found wide acceptance within industry. There are many good ones available, such as the Personal Profile System (DISC) , the Myers-Briggs, or Kolbe systems. The most useful insight from these assessment tools is that people are different in somewhat predictable ways. If we can learn how they are different, and more importantly how they prefer to be treated, and treat them as they prefer while we collaborate, we can make more progress.

Team stage differences can be described with the Stage Theory: "Form, Storm, Norm, Perform" model (as first described by B.W. Tuckman). In "forming" the team assembles and does a lot of weather talk. They are just getting used to each other. In "storming" the team begins to do work and there is some lighting and thunder as the team encounters differences of opinion. In "norming" the team learns to handle the differences, often yielding to accommodating, compromising, and/or competing behaviors and decisions (still a suboptimal endpoint). In performing, the team has learned to optimize the differences of opinions, and even to create/provoke different options to broaden their choices. They have very likely learned to collaborate productively.

The concept of stages in change initiatives is illustrated by the four-room apartment model of Claes Janssen. Similar to a standard grief series of emotional states, Dr. Janssen suggests that we start with denial, move through confusion and renewal before arriving at contentment. We can appreciate differences within the team when we appreciate that people move through these stages with any change initiative, at their own rate.

While appreciating personal differences, team-development stage differences, and change initiative-stage differences, it is important that the team not skip any stage or step in its process to avoid these differences. We must be patient as our team develops as fast as it can through these stages. That may not always be as fast as some team members want to move, but it is as fast as possible without derailing a meeting. Taking time for team growth is not an excuse for inactivity: the team must be persistent about its progress.

Team development can be accelerated by learning and practicing collaboration skills. As mentioned before, active collaboration does not require a careful unpacking of individual differences. As a musician, I don't need to know all the psychological details of another musician I'm playing with. The music, the product, is a result of what we do together. If we collaborate we can do something great. If we fall into conflict or compromise we choose to be mediocre. Which band would you prefer to be part of?

The Roadblocks of Personal Differences

Personal differences can be merely speed bumps, slowing the team's progress but manageable with collaboration tools and techniques. When conflicts are based on misunderstandings about issues or communication, a conscientious collaboration will unravel the confusion. The key is that all parties want the same thing (to solve the problem at hand), and are all open to the same solution (they just haven't discovered it yet).

Collaboration tools can also dismantle misunderstandings when two parties have the same needs but different co-operative options. For example, consider two people arguing over who gets an orange. They both want it–in fact, they both need it to achieve their objectives. They are both convinced that if the other person gets the orange they will be unable to complete their task. They could just argue (conflict), or compromise (each of them gets half of the orange). But through a data-driven dialogue process

<20</20>

(which brings data to the surface) they discover that one wants the rind to make a pie, the other wants the center to make some juice. There was no reason for conflict or compromise: each one can have what they need.

But not all differences are speed bumps: some are roadblocks, and collaboration tools and techniques cannot always overcome them. Sometimes people have mutually exclusive needs and non-cooperative options (both want the orange, for the same reasons, and want to make sure that the other one doesn't get it). These sorts of "zero sum games" are unfortunate, and they happen far too frequently. Should you encounter this type of competition, try to redirect it by having the parties involved generate one (and only one) scoreboard of the goals that they all can support. If that is impossible and the team is split along these sort of lines, someone may have to leave the team. These roadblocks are often the seeds of war.

Moving Forward Together

Collaboration is often wrongly labelled groupthink, but nothing could be farther from the truth. In fact, the two are opposite concepts. Collaborators are searching for new ideas, and are not particularly attached to their own if they find something better. Groupthink is a reduction of options down to the lowest common denominator. The group's identity is wrapped up in some idea or approach, and the members of the group are absorbed into it. Groupthink exhibits no curiosity, just conformity.

Hunger for and curiosity about new ideas factor heavily into whether a team will successfully collaborate. If people aren't hungry, they won't bother to search for or grow their own food. If people aren't looking for new ideas, they won't find any. Dr. Alan Robinson states that, "It is a universal truth that those who are not dissatisfied will never make any progress." Risk-averse company cultures have a full spectrum of, "Been there, done that" idioms in use to discourage new ideas and their enthusiastic thinkers.

Fear of change is a current that collaborating teams must paddle against. But if the team accepts that it needs new products and services to be competitive, then it must constantly improve. To improve it must change, it must start doing something new, and stop doing something old. Ideally, the team wants to change and improve faster than its competitors.

Moving forward as a team to discover solutions should be easy. Reducing or eliminating the constraints makes new options available.

In the case of people stuck on their positions, initiating structured dialogue is an opportunity for the team members to see things differently. Dialogue is an interactive conversation or experience that generates new knowledge.

As we said, hunger for new ideas is a vital quality in a team searching for them. We all get motivated to make changes when we see an obvious difference between what we have and what we want to have. A scoreboard tool, with real, objective numbers reflecting actual performance against goals, can make a team hungry for change. The team can elevate its goals by benchmarking its objectives with a visit to another organization that is demonstrating what's possible. These are great learning opportunities for leaders and employees. On the ride home, the team says to each other, "Wow, we could do that, and better!"

The "Discussability of the Undiscussed"

Lots of employees privately describe their company as dysfunctional. Nasty, unproductive behaviors are sources of waste right along with Taiichi Ohno's famous seven sources of waste. In some companies it's acceptable to actively and deliberately pursue factory and process waste, but it's not OK to talk about waste-behaviors. Just how serious is an organization that says it really wants to be profitable, and a great place to work, but doesn't want to and/or cannot talk about the real source of the dysfunctional behaviors that keep it from reaching those goals?

Some years ago, Charlotte Roberts (coauthor of *The Fifth Discipline Fieldbook* and others works on change management) introduced me to a wonderfully mind contorting phrase: "Can we discuss the discussability of the undiscussed?" She meant that within most organizations some topics are taboo: we cannot talk about them. But that undermines our search for better options. Some of our behavior, and the thinking which drives it, is off-limits to any conversation or evaluation. Considering the enormous cost of dysfunction, this may be the next organizational performance frontier.

If we don't talk about our patterns of thinking, what do we talk about? Improving morale? Having a very entertaining offsite or spectacular hour-long keynote speaker? Or shall we move the horse in front of the cart and deliberately have the tough (?) conversations about how leaders think, deliberately improve their performance, and then celebrate.

I am not suggesting that we have these tough conversations in an unstructured way. Process and structure allow the team members to consider and build positive alternatives while not falling into careless and emotional volleys. I am suggesting (pleading) that having these conversations in a productive way may be one of the most important improvement strategies an organization can implement. If we improve the leadership, then we improve the organization's capacity to improve.

3
Resolving Conflict, Resolving Options

How We Think About Conflict: A Real Fork in the Road

> *I shall be telling this with a sigh*
> *Somewhere ages and ages hence:*
> *Two roads diverged in a wood, and I,*
> *I took the one less travelled by,*
> *And that has made all the difference*

– Robert Frost, Business Philosopher

Boy, did Frost get this right! Everyone talks about conflict in the workplace. Too many know how to make it go away by squashing it. Too many have learned to live with it, but not like it.

How one thinks about conflict and all the associated emotions, and how one manages their reactions to the conflict, can "make all the difference." This chapter may give you the keys to thinking in a way that makes you and your business perform better than ever before.

Conflict – A Real Growth Industry

Roger Fisher and William Ury (of the Harvard Negotiation Project) speak with wisdom and practical perspective in their book *Getting to Yes*. They address the ever growing attraction in our society to conflict – here meaning when two or more people actively and publicly share their very different points of view. In fact, as Fisher and Ury observe, "Conflict is definitely a growth industry."

And share, and share, and share – selling all sorts of newspapers, tabloids, movies, reality TV programs, political analysis, etc etc. This kind of conflict is demonstrated by behaviors and decisions that most often defend (and defend, and defend) a person's point of view.

I suspect that you have experienced and do experience what you think of as conflict in your workplace. It has many forms. It most often involves some friction between two or more people, overt or covert. Some types that I have survived within my career include: passive aggressive (when people say one thing but do another), pulling rank ("I'm making the decision because of my position"), exaggeration to win others over ("Almost everyone wants to do it my way"), coming to meetings late and/or unprepared, too little dialogue before decisions, and many others.

Notice that conflict is present anytime opposing forces become evident. You're pushing an idea one way and someone else enters into the fray and pushes in a different direction. Sporting comparisons are obvious. Work comparisons may be more subtle. The sporting world makes millions capitalizing on sporting conflict. You can learn to capitalize on business conflict when you learn to think about it productively. Read on.

EXERCISE
Conflict Report: Experience Review

Bring life to this topic by creating your own real list of forms of conflict that you experience in the workplace.

Working alone or with other participants, document and discuss the conflict you experience in your organization.

I will suggest you complete this exercise with a flip chart sheet and some Post-Its. This will provide a large and flexible format to do your work.

1. Silently brainstorm the forms of conflict from your work,writing one idea per Post-It. Come up with ten if you're working alone, or five per person if working with a team.

2. Meet with your team participants at a flip chart sheet at a stand or on the wall.

3. Presenting one idea at a time, move around your circle until everyone has discussed and posted all their ideas. Do not pre-sort the Post-Its.

4. Silently organize the random Post-its into groups of similar topics.

5. Discuss, title, and prioritize the groups of Post-Its by impact on your organization's success.

6. Discuss your findings; themes, principles, processes, etc.

You have created a list of customer complaints which your collaboration skills should address. You can also change the bias of the information to the positive (do that which eliminates these problems) and you will have a list of goals for your collaboration skills initiative.

Mountain or a Molehill?

Back to the issue of conflict. Does it affect performance in the workplace? Does it affect employee morale? Does it matter?

Your reaction will likely depend on how you have come to think about this conflict – the behaviors that get in the way of progress. If you grew up with the rule, "If you don't have anything nice to say, then be silent," then you are likely a contributor to artificial harmony. You may spend time every day in "the second meeting" talking about other meetings and what should have happened, who should have said what, what you'd do if you were in charge.

From Another Point of View

Many successful companies have learned to think about their manufacturing and service activities as processes, and the process problems in terms of waste. Toyota has helped us learn to think about waste in terms of *The Seven Sources of Waste:*

Taiichi Ohno Seven Sources of Waste

1. Overproduction
   - too much of the right products or services
   - extra work
2. Waiting
   - delayed action
   - forgetting
3. Inventory
   - work-in-process
   - deteriorating products or services
   - un-used training
4. Unnecessary Processing
   - too many steps
   - no added value

5. Transportation
   - excessive time or distance between stations
6. Motion within work station
   - in our day-to-day jobs
7. Defects, errors

These improvement efforts target the ten to thirty percent of an organization's revenue that is being spent on generating waste. This waste is often hiding in their company processes. Employees and leaders must learn to see the waste, and then reduce/eliminate it.

Waste is a Crime

This improvement approach has provided companies with a taxonomy to think about, describe, target, and eliminate work that does not add value: waste.

What's key here is that it's now O.K. to talk about these issues. Teams now have a way to talk about the elephant in the living room: the waste that they may experience everyday in the work place. Historically they had no way to talk about the issues, and thus no way to address and repair the problems.

Significantly, in targeting the processes that contribute to the waste, there is a reduced opportunity for leaders and employees to think about and talk about egos and personalities. There is a reduced need for anyone to behave defensively, since we're talking about the process, not people's quirks and shortcomings.

Part of the journey down the road less traveled asks you to consider the many forms of conflict, most often a myriad of unhelpful behaviors in the workplace, as waste. In manufacturing and service processes, any steps that do not add value can be considered waste. Many of these companies claim to be saving many millions of dollars in the doing.

Waste is not only a big deal, removing it is very profitable. Improvements often do not require capital expense. Many effective improvement teams efforts provide double digit rates of return, and as such, are great investment strategies.

The point is that to not address and work to eliminate waste and defects, when this perspective and help is available, can be considered a crime. It is stealing money by allowing suboptimal processes to waste money, to the tune of ten to thirty percent of an organization's revenues.

Waste & Crime Perpetrated

Part of my client work includes many keynote speeches throughout the year. In these presentations, I get a chance to ask questions and get a quick audience response. So while their reactions are not hard scientific data, I do notice some trends worthy of mention.

One question I've been asking is, "How many of you work in organizations that can deliberately solve a problem, i.e. deliberately improve a process?" In other words, how many of your organizations have improvement teams that use a structured improvement process (PDCA, 8 D's, Kepner Trego, etc.) to guide their thinking past the emotional and personality-based opinions to solid data-supported options. They can identify possible root causes, conduct experiments to confirm the offending process steps, and successfully implement the improved processes where applicable.

I should add that my audiences are primarily operational leaders from service and manufacturing companies, large and small. Usually there are somewhere between fifty and ninety in attendance: project managers, operation managers, HR leaders–people who have direct responsibility for leading the processes that determine a company's success.

To the question about a company-wide, or even group-local, improvement capability being in place and used, only about ten percent of the audience raises their hands.

So, considering the numbers, if we estimate that any organization not deliberately improving their processes is likely spending ten to thirty percent of their revenues generating waste—wow, that's a lot of waste!

Let's translate this into work hours. Assuming eight hours in the work day and fifty-two weeks in the year, there are 2,080 hours a year per employee. With even ten percent waste, each employee may be spending about two hundred hours per year not adding value; just going about their business, responding to requests—you know, day-to-day stuff. Divided by forty hours a week, that's five wasted weeks per year. It's sort of like an extra and very long paid vacation for every worker.

Another Form of Waste: Dysfunctional Behaviors

Reconsidering the forms of conflict listed earlier in this chapter, yours and mine, please consider the behaviors that do not help as waste. Many of these behaviors would easily be considered dysfunctional, especially in the context of the accumulated effect in a meeting.

For simplicity, I like to categorize just about any list of dysfunctional behaviors into columns with four possible headers: avoid, accommodate, compromise, and compete.

You will learn as you read that I do not seem to need to eliminate the dysfunctional behaviors, I just need to replace them with collaboration.

COLLABORATE

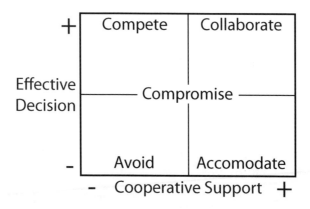

My first book, *Think or Sink: A Parable of Collaboration,* provides an overview example of what happens to employees who are led by both competitive or accommodating leaders. Louise, the "competer," has everyone on pins and needles as she uses a series of threats to "motivate" her team to help her climb the corporate ladder. Mark, the "accomodater," has many on his team bored and aimless as few decisions get made with enough integrity or timeliness to make a difference. Employees on both teams share their angst as the story progresses.

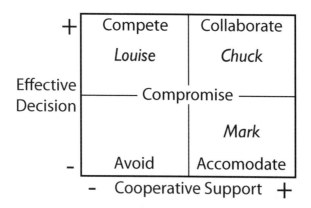

Scene of the Crime

Many of the conflicts and behaviors that we experience are expressed when we are gathered together to generate, consider, and select options – i.e. to make decisions.

The vast majority of decision-making worldwide is conducted through meetings, the title of the social forum we use to describe these collections of people assembled for a purpose.

As such, meetings are one of the spots to learn to use more effective collaboration techniques and tools.

Meetings are where most of our work gets done. They're very important. They cannot and should not be eliminated. They should be a primary target for our improvement efforts. If you consider a meeting as a decision making factory, modern improvement thinking would ask are your meetings waste and defect free?

If not, improve the process—read chapter seven and build a much improved meeting process for you and your team..

Inside the Box

Now to address the source of the conflict.

Considering the word pair: "conflict" and "resolution." I once wondered if conflict were a chemical compound and I resolved it, i.e. broke it down to its component elements, what would I find? So similarly picture yourself at a non-productive meeting, lots of conflict. Why is there conflict present? Why are people challenging others? What is it they are challenging? What's the conflict stuff all about?

Not to be simplistic, but there wouldn't be any conflict if everyone agreed. So it seems that the conflict is present when people discover they do not agree. Considering the many ways people can be different, it is upon consideration, no surprise there is conflict. In fact if I'm really pursuing people's real views on issues, especially at the beginning of an initiative, I would/should be surprised if I didn't see conflict.

So conflict is just the discovery of different points of view. No big deal. Just to know how to think about it. Just know how to work with it.

Digging Deeper: The DNA of Conflict

When I consider thinking drives ideas, and ideas drive behavior, I want to know what's driving the dysfunctional behavior. How is this person thinking that they behave that way?

After all they are likely behaving in a way they think serves their interests and goals. They're doing the best job they know how to help what they want to achieve.

Here we need to consider the always-present issue of how a person sees (thinks about) their own point of view versus the other options that might be available to consider when moving towards a decision making situation. I find this a significant fork in the road. People heading down one route are less collaborative than those who head down the other route.

Here's how I think about this: Some people grow up thinking that the way they see things, is the way things are. "Everyone is entitled to my opinion," "My way or the highway," etc. And they think they are their idea. They very much personalize the idea with the owner—themselves. You've seen this in the workplace when someone's idea is challenged and they take it personally and as a result behave defensively. It is hard for these thinkers to collaborate unless their idea is confirmed. They act like soccer goalies trying to keep any and all new ideas out of their "net". From *Think or Sink,* Louise and similar thinkers are addicted to being right; Mark and similar thinkers are addicted to being liked.

Alternatively people can learn to think that their point of view is merely a current alternative. One of many options. May the best idea win. Let me repeat that: May the best idea win, not just "me".

I consider the recognition of alternative points of view as conflict. And with all the different people being different in many ways, there is a lot of conflict around.

The big deal here is how we think about the conflict. If we think conflict is bad – unpleasant, not helpful, noisy, unpredictable—just generally nasty—we will likely avoid it. But, if we step back from a conflict-situation and consider what's going on, we may notice the reason there is conflict is because people have different points of view. What else is new?

So, if we can in our thinking see that the conflict is merely this point of recognizing different points of view, we can learn to not avoid it like the plague. Alternatively, significantly, when we can learn to see the conflict as an opportunity that includes options to choose from we may even want to promote/provoke the number of options we have to choose from. Entering a Baskin & Robbins ice cream shop creates conflict: there are thirty-one different choices–oh what to do. A nice problem to have.

The lucky ones at some point have a turning point experience that allows them to actually appreciate conflict.

Mine came many years ago as I began work as an engineer at Intel in Santa Clara, I had read *The 100 Best Companies to Work for in America* by Levering and Moskowitz. In the top margin of Intel's chapter it listed phrases that best described the work environment. Out from the page jumped "They yell at each other a lot." Ugh, what have I gotten myself into? After all, I had grown up in the Midwest (Madison, Wis.) where I learned if you didn't have something nice to say, well, just don't say it all.

After arriving at Intel, and getting to work in the first few months at one point I began to notice and listen to the "yelling." Importantly, this level of verbal exchange was largely impersonal — it was about wafer yields, making production deliveries, passing qualification tests, and making some money. Intel was/is not a polite place. But neither is any sporting venue when the players and the fans really care about what's going on.

To review, how individuals react to conflict depends how they think about conflict. In *Think or Sink*, if a person like Louise thinks they have the right answer, pretty much all the time, when someone challenges their point of view, they will react defensively. Why? They think they're defending themselves, and because it works too often. These folks get their way.

Others, like Mark, are often confused about the defensive behavior and back off and avoid, accommodate, or compromise their own points of view just to quiet the situation. This is often called artificial harmony.

In summary, be aware of the poor decisions and behavior a leader is exhibiting, and target their thinking. Help them to think differently to generate new ideas that drive improved decisions and support.

Wasteful Behaviors Perpetrated

Back in July 2009 my MiBiz article (Michigan Business News, www.mibiz.com, "Good Thinking") *What Are They Thinking?* I wrote about Charlotte Roberts' *Discussability of the Undiscussed*. The article solicited some responses from a number of people. This article outlined a structured methodology to uncover the helpful and not-so-helpful behaviors and driving thinking of individual leaders.

These responders thought it would take a really strong team, a team willing to take risks, to actually complete an exercise like this. In other years-past conversations I have had leaders clarify how someone thinks is their own business - you can't talk about that.

One of my primary insights after 10 years in industry (Intel and Herman Miller) and 20 years as an independent consultant around the world is that thinking drives performance. As I introduced in Chapter 1:

Improved Company Performance
↑
Improved Decisions & Support
↑
Improved Ideas
↑
Improved Thinking

If this is close to true, considering the thinking that a leader uses is considering the DNA of their leadership and its effect on an organization.

You could target behaviors and ask the suspect not to use them, but if you haven't provided an opportunity for the suspect to select new thinking, their behavior is likely to stay the same.

4

Productive Collaboration Fundamental Strategy

Do Nothing or Do Something

After deciding that you want to collaborate in your workplace, your next task is to learn how to be deliberately collaborative, and to use collaboration tools to help individuals and teams develop productive dialogue and make and support better decisions. There are many good ways and resources available to learn to develop collaboration skills and use collaboration tools.

Let's quickly compare a collaborative and a non collaborative approach.

Let's say I want to solve a problem: I want to improve what I'm doing, right now. In a random approach, I will assemble a team and brainstorm what the team members think the problem is. I end up with lots of talk and lots of options.

In a collaborative approach, we meet around a flip chart and create a flowchart starting with the last step: the problem. We then discuss and document what we know to be the preceding steps, going to the workplace to confirm our perceptions. Once we have what we believe to be an accurate description of the problem and the contributing process, we then wonder together which step is the most likely to include the possible root cause. We conduct an experiment to confirm our guess. If we find the cause, we modify the process step, and make the problem go away.

In another example, if I'm not satisfied with the options that I have available, I do not rely solely on brainstorming. I use collaboration tools like Mind Mapping or Random Word that deliberately provoke neural associations that generate new insights. In Strategic Planning, I ask about ten great questions that, answered by a thoughtful leadership team, develop a course of action that the team will support. Scenario Planning, a real brain burner, asks teams to consider four alternative futures and think through how they would thrive or survive in each. I will cover these topics in more depth in the third and fourth books in the *Good Thinking Series* (*Plan* and *Imagine*).

The point here is that if I want great decisions supported by the whole team, I need to structure the best way for the team to think and learn, and identify and buy into new options. This might happen accidentally, but it might not. Once a person knows how to use collaboration tools effectively, and keep learning new ones, they can help lead a team to build both better decisions while they help develop better support.

We have a choice: Make it happen, or let it happen. Think or sink.

Consider the difference between dialogue vs. discussion. With dialogue team members actively listen to understand others' points of view, and speak to describe their point of view while working to build a common understanding. Dialogue can describe the kind of conversation which builds a synergistic new and better understanding of an issue. Discussion describes the kind of conversation which only presents and compares current points of view. Without any work to identify a common set of goals, there will be competition between different sets of goals—all too often unspoken.

To me the key difference is the shortage of meaningful dialogue in the non-collaborative example. The non-collaborative conversation just wanders. One or two people will probably lead the discussion, and the decision. Without the dialogue, there is very little learning, just a competitive series of opinions. Without dialogue there's little opportunity to build buy-in.

Effective Collaboration has Two Crucial Components

As introduced in Chapter One, one is to ask the team to identify the best alternative—to make a really good decision. Good meetings actively promote identifying and prioritizing best choices often hiding in a wide variety of strongly-held personal opinions. Sometimes it's adequate to just brainstorm and select. But at other times teams need to get past the "politically correct" speed bumps and get the water cooler issues on the table so they too can be considered. And still other times, the best ideas haven't been discovered yet.

A crucial second component is to deliberately build support for the team's selections by organizing the dialogue to promote participant contribution and buy-in. Here we want to take advantage of the wonderful principle that people support what they help create. When people are included in the identification, comparison, and selection of alternatives, most often a very good solution emerges which everyone can support.

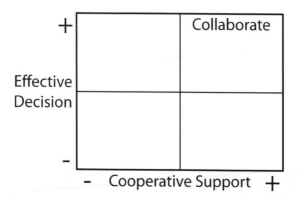

It is this combination of both better decisions and better support that provides team decisions which generate significant business impact.

Consolidate the Differences

As I mentioned in a previous chapter, we could think about all this in far more complicated ways, but would it be useful? I think not. While there are many reasons people may not collaborate, what is refreshing is that you don't have to deal with all the personal differences. I consolidate the differences into the five behaviors: avoiders, accomodaters, compromisers, competers, and collaborators (borrowed from the Thomas Kilmann model:

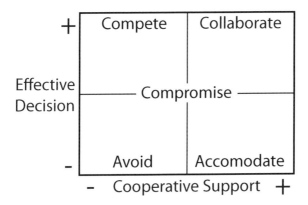

The behavior options, in this model introduced back in chapter three, include:

- **Avoiders** don't really want to help and have few good ideas. They often say "I really can't' help now, sorry". Nothing gets done. Risk-phobia at work.

- **Accommodators** are just in it for the fun of being together with others. When it's time to make a decision they say " Whatever you say, I'm just glad to help in any way." Driven by a need for social affirmation. "I just want to be liked...."

- The **Compromisers** haven't learned to expect more. They settle for half a good decision and half the buy-in that might be developed. Their motto is "I can live with that." A lazy stopping point.

- The **Competers** would rather do all this themselves. Their mantra is "My way or the highway". Stop signs are for other people. Competers often have good ideas but when they're railroaded through teams, the lack of support, or resistance, minimizes or eliminates the benefit.

COLLABORATE

Our goal, collaborating, is different. Collaborating is all about learning a better way with a group. With these folks, when they have two options, they've learned the best is always the third. Collaborating is a key business communication strategy to both improve and innovate.

Settling for less than collaboration is a business decision, and often not a very good one.

Looking at your Chapter Three Exercise (Conflict Review) flip chart, which problems could be described by which "optional behavior?"

EXERCISE
Thinking, Behavior, and Business Impact Options

The following exercise will help you understand the differences between these behaviors, and the business impact of each.

1. Working alone or with your team mates, document and discuss each of five behavior options (avoid, accommodate, compromise, compete, or collaborate) one at a time.

2. List the behaviors, thinking, and business results in three columns on a different flip chart. The behavior is what you see happening when this option is being expresses. The thinking drives the behavior in question. The business results asks you to think back to similar situations and speculate how this particular pair of thinking and behavior affects business.

Behaviors	Thinking	Business Results
Example: *Compete* aggressive defensive wording, body language,	"I'm the only one who really knows what's going on and what to do..."	Incomplete buy-in... competition for resources...low morale

3. Discuss your findings; themes, principles, processes, etc.

One summary of this exercise would encourage you to appreciate that the dysfunctional behaviors are not just unpleasant – they have a significant negative financial and emotional impact on the business. Using appropriate tools correctly tends to pull groups up into the collaborating corner.

Collaboration Skills – Mindset "Operating system" for Collaborators:

So, some more detail on how collaborators look at the world, how they think.

Business performance improvement depends on making and supporting better decisions. Decisions can be made by either one person or a team. The vast majority of decisions are implemented by teams. To maximize the impact of these decisions, we want to maximize the contribution each team member is willing and able to make in helping to implement the decision. We can do this by training and expecting team members to work as a team to build decisions each member wants to support.

Part of this training can include some new/review considerations of the "software code" we use in our thinking:

Some Helpful Ways to Think:

- **Point of View:** a person's particular way of looking at things, their paradigm, their position. Our paradigms are the result of the interaction of our conditioned perceptual skills and reinforced experiences.

- **Conflict:** discovery of different points of view.

- **Challenge:** an impersonal request to consider an alternative point of view.

- **Shared Understanding:** an improved understanding of the breadth and depth of an issue as a result of dialogue.

- **Equifinality:** the notion that there is not only one way to do something, but rather a number of ways which, successfully supported, will generate an acceptable result. Our goal is to pick a good one, and deliberately make it a success.

- **Collaboration:** the opposite of avoiding Collaborating involves an attempt to work with the other people to find some solution which fully satisfies the concerns of all persons. It means digging into an issue to identify the underlying concerns of the individuals and to find and alternative which meets the concerns. Collaborating might take the form of exploring a disagreement to learn from others' insights, concluding to resolve some condition which would otherwise have them competing for resources, or confronting and trying to find a creative solution to an interpersonal problem.

- **Dialogue vs. Discussion:** Team members actively listen to understand others' points of view, and speak to describe their point of view while working to build a shared understanding. Dialogue can describe the kind of conversation which builds a synergistic new and better understanding of an issue. Discussion describes the kind of conversation which only presents and compares current points of view.

- **Contribution vs. Participation:** Team members contribute to building team decisions when they actively listen to understand others' points of view, and speak to describe their point of view while owning being responsible for ending with a decision they will actively support. Team members who participate only attend meetings and are happy when the team makes a decision they can live with.

- **Insights:** the "ah ha's" which occur often in dialogue when we begin to see either an old or new issue in a different way. This new way of looking at things often frees us to respect and incorporate others' points of view for ourselves.

- **Disagree but Commit:** Occasionally, a team member will not come to see an issue as the team does, even after numerous presentations of data. We can optimize the impact of this team by asking this team member to accept they do not agree with the team on this issue, but fully support the decision of the team while registering their own position. And actively support, not just "live with."

- **Tools:** Productive dialogue requires the presentation of different points of view and substantiation with data when possible. Tools allow the team to physically place the issue out in front of the group, while minimizing distracting personality issues. Tools help teams build and support great decisions. These tools provide the participants a chance to document what's really happening and to question if the current picture is accurate. The charts and diagrams also provide a neutral, physical focal point for the participants to look. It serves the critical function of breaking eye-to-eye contact and disarming the fight or flight instinct.

People are far more likely to move into an unproductive argument if they are making a lot of eye contact and intent on protecting their position and status. For example, imagine two couples are lost in a strange city, one with a map and one without. The couple without a map look at each other and bicker. The one with a map spread it out, point to it, and ask, "Let's see, where are we?" The simple act of making people look at data physically displayed in a neutral location can further dialogue, and thus collaboration.

Collaboration Skills Strategy – Executive Summary

Thirty years of experience inside and outside of many great companies has led me to the following view of how company performance is driven:

Improved Company Performance
↑
Improved Decisions & Support
↑
Improved Ideas
↑
Improved Thinking

So if I really want to improve my performances, what is the best way to think about it.

One very helpful distinction I learned first from Edward de Bono's books: intelligence and thinking are different. Intelligence is capability, like the hard disk in a computer, and thinking is how you use it, like the software managing your hard disk. Thinking, then, is a skill, and as such is improvable.

Productive collaboration deliberately guides the thinking of a team's members by providing tools that guide the thinking for a period of time.

For example, in a problem solving situation, a non-collaborative team will likely sit in a circle at a table, talk around the possible causes, look to find someone to blame, and try some stuff to make the problem go away. A collaborative team would follow their Improvement Process (a recipe of collaborative steps and tools) starting with a flow chart as a brainstorming format to list what they know to be happening with the process, not just the people.

Other tools help the team to identify and prioritize possible root causes, conduct experiments to test possibilities, and likely nail the cause by learning what is really happening with the process. Without the tools to guide the team's thinking, the team would likely spend far more time with far less to show for it.

The collaboration tools do not tell team members what

to think, but how.

The tools are fundamentally great questions. Questions answered openly and honestly, with the help of data, in the company of the team members generates dialogue and learning.

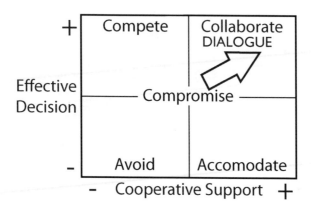

Effective collaboration pulls the team member behaviors towards collaborate, minimizing/eliminating the effect of the non-collaborative behaviors.

The facilitator role here is to know which tool will best provide the learning necessary to help the team make progress.

Collaboration Skills Strategy – Why This Works

You might consider that there are three types of thinking:

- **Instinctive:** you decide "automatically" - you pin prick your finger and your hand moves away.

- **Emotional:** you decide based on how it feels at the moment. "Oh, one more cookie is not going to hurt." This type of thinking uses the amygdala of your brain

- **Intelligent:** you decide based on a comparison of your current options against your documented goals. This type of thinking engages the prefrontal cortex of your brain, where the "executive functioning" takes place.

You may have heard of an "Amygdala Highjack" where you make a decision emotionally at the moment, but come to regret it and want to reverse as you think more about it —i.e. when you engage your intelligent thinking.

The fundamental purpose of effective collaboration is to keep you and your team thinking intelligently as often as possible. The techniques and tools promote/provoke intelligent thinking by engaging the prefrontal cortex by asking great questions. When the team answers these questions while together, they will far more likely build better decisions and better buy-in.

The barriers to collaboration are rarely physical. They are most often emotional. They are best dealt with by addressing the thinking that drives the emotions.

So in summary, as introduced in Chapter 1, effective collaboration:

- **Is deliberate.** It does not happen accidently or randomly.
- **Builds better options** by comparing data to listed goals.
- **Builds buy-in** by being so interactive allowing each team member to be heard (people support what they help create.

- **Works best when the team uses effective tools** which guide a team's thinking in a very interactive way.

Summer Rip Currents

Every summer, on windy days in Lake Michigan, some people get caught by those nasty rip currents, the strong water currents that can carry swimmers away from shore. Rip currents are a natural phenomenon – they happen, and as such, are predictable if you know about them.

If you don't know about rip currents, you could panic, try to swim directly against them, and make it to shore if you're lucky. If you've learned about rip currents, you know to swim along the shore awhile, and then head for the beach encountering much reduced or no currents moving out. A simple idea that could save your life.

In the case of collaboration, your mature appreciation of conflict (there are some options here to harvest !) and knowing what to do (use collaboration tools to identify better ideas that people support) instead of letting yourself get hijacked by your emotions, can allow you to help you and your team accomplish solid goals when some others, thinking less effectively, would only fail and give up.

Learn to lead down the path less traveled. Think or sink.

5
Smaller Group Collaboration Techniques

The primary purpose of the Good Thinking Series of books is to help individuals and teams improve their performance by guiding their thinking to make better decisions and build better buy-in.

Improved Company Performance

↑

Improved Decisions & Support

↑

Improved Ideas

↑

Improved Thinking

So while it is very important to wonder, "If I really want to improve my performance, what's the best way to think about this? This can be focused as, "Which tool should I use to guide my thinking?" I also want to keep myself focused by asking "What decision should I make next to move me towards my goals?"

Someone once joked "You can't not decide." Say you end a meeting by saying, "Let's not decide today." Well, you just did decide—to delay the decision. If there is a time value to the decision you probably could calculate how much the delay will cost, like not depositing some money in an interest bearing account, losing the accumulative value of the earlier decision.

The decision is the stepping-stone to action. No decision, no action.

My purpose in this and the next chapter is not to attempt to present a comprehensive collection of all, or even many, of the collaboration techniques available. There are many good resources of techniques and tools. What I do hope to do is to help inspire (or encourage) you to use techniques and tools like those in this and the next chapter.

It is not even interesting if someone knows how to use lots and lots of tools, but does not put them to use for themselves or their teams. As James Belasco notes, "Leadership is not about what you know, it's about what you do with what you know."

The most effective way to learn this collaboration approach is to actually use the tools in either a seminar situation or a real work situation. Just reading will be interesting, but until you use a tool to direct the thinking, modify/improve the options, and modify/improve the decisions and support, you won't see and feel the improved results. I recommend people practice with groups out of work – non-profits, school meetings, church meetings, family meetings. The better practiced you are when you present this approach to a work team, the more likely they will welcome your help. The more likely you as a helpful messenger won't be shot.

And while I have organized the following tools in a Smaller Group chapter, you are encouraged to try any of these and other techniques not only with larger groups, but also with yourself as you work by yourself working to make better decisions that you like better.

The tools I will present are pretty easy to use and likely

to be used occasionally to frequently. They are most often used in groups of 2-4, and often used when the decisions to be made are about relationships and expectations between people.

- Need a team?
- Communication process
- AB See
- SMARTR

1. Need a Team?

Now this may be obvious, but often the decisions you need to make don't require someone else's help – for information and/or support. So this quick little pair of questions can help you move ahead quicker by working alone when it's appropriate:

Do you have the information you need to make a decision? If yes move on alone, if no assemble a team that can help you.

Do you have the support you need to make the decision a success? If yes move on alone, if no assemble a team that can help you.

2. Communication process skills

We know that communication between people can be complicated. This series of paragraphs is only intended to remind you that you have to decide what happens when there is effective communication.

One common model includes the following steps and sub-steps:

- Connecting: Building rapport, adapting, and using eye contact.
- Encouraging: Reinforcing, empathizing, accepting.
- Questioning: Open questioning.
- Confirming: Summarizing , checking.
- Providing: Stating benefits, speaking concisely, using enthusiasm.

Common supporting suggestions include:

- Listen actively and acknowledge what has been said
- Speak to be understood. What method will be best received ?
- Speak about yourself, not them. "I feel let down," not, "You cheated me!"
- Speak for a purpose; Speak only if there is value to speaking.
- Manage your emotions
- Recognize your and their emotions
- Make emotions explicit/acknowledge as legitimate
- Allow other side to let off steam
- Don't react to emotional outbursts
- Use symbolic gestures such as an apology

I suspect that this book's readers have been through a workshop on a method like this. While I am not going to dig into this process, in the spirit of continuous improvement, I would suggest that you bother to document your preferred communication process and repeatedly wonder if it's working for you as well as it might.

I recommend not having a set sequence to the steps above, but rather choose to use each step as necessary, and using each step at least one time in each meeting.

What is your definition of a good communication? For the purpose of this book series, mine is when dialogue supports individuals and teams to build great decisions with great support. Use whatever it takes–communication, dialogue– to exchange information and everything else between people.

All the dialogue techniques and tools here, the other *Good Thinking Series* books, and elsewhere are alternative strategies to support effective communication.

3. AB See

"Did you hear what I think I said?"

AB See is a collaboration tool best used when two parties too often move to argument and rarely accomplish anything.

The goal is to establish dialogue. In dialogue all members actively listen to understand others' points of view, and speak to describe their point of view while working to build a shared understanding. Dialogue can describe the kind of conversation which builds a synergistic new and better understanding of an issue.

Ordinary discussion describes the kind of conversation which often only presents and compares current points of view. If positions and/or personalities are strong, it usually deteriorates to an argument.

AB See Exercise Instructions

- Assemble two opposing persons in a room with a third person as a referee just in case things get testy.
- Decide which opposing person is A and B
- Flip a coin to decide who goes first, let's say A.
- A speaks while B can only listen while B take notes.
- When A says they're done, B must report what they heard A said without any editing etc. When B is done, A must confirm B heard A. If not, B continues.
- Reverse roles and repeat.

The beauty and effectiveness of this simple technique is that its structure when followed by the participants prevents an argument, maximizing the chance to be heard as well as hear.

In my experience, about 70% of the formerly arguing parties come to discover they had only a misunderstanding significantly improving their willingness and ability to work together in the future more productively.

4. SMARTR

S: Specific
M: Measurable
A: Accountable
R: Realistic.
T: Time bound
R: Resources

Use this tool to clarify many/most of the components

of the of an initiative. The work can be completed on a sheet of paper, or on a flip chart filling in the data on Post-Its.

One great application is to use this tool as a brainstorming format which the employee and the supervisor fill out together. Both parties get heard. Let the employee lead the dialogue. You may find they set higher goals than you as a leader might have.

The purpose of this tool is to guide the dialogue to help the two parties learn and document what each really needs to know to feel confident that the project can be started and completed without a lot of micromanaging by the leader. The SMARTR are intended to provide a fairly comprehensive listing of what each party would want to know.

Add any criteria you'd want to see. I've added the last R, resources:

SMARTR with my preferred definitions

  S: Stretch: Will this project help us attain new significant levels of performance?

  M: Measurable: Is data available to objectively measure our starting point, monitor the project, and confirm successful completion?

  A: Aligned: Does this project support the current company objectives and strategies?

  R: Realistic; How feasible is success for this initiative?

  T: Time bound: When will the project be done?

  R: Resources: What (capital, cash, materials, people, etc.) will it take to complete this task?

A similar format from Intel went: *who* will do *what* by *when, with* success as measured by what?

In any case, determine the criteria for a well described project *with* the other party, and work together to fill it in. The format's questions will lead your dialogue.

Smaller Group Collaboration Techniques Tips

These tools are most often used between two or three people, a smaller group. And as luck would have it because interpersonal issues often occur at this level, versus larger group, these tools are often used to redirect or diffuse unhelpful emotional situations that occur between people.

I also recommend if you find yourself apprehensive about a meeting, find another person you know to role play the discussion a few times before you begin the conversation with the person you really want to talk with. This builds both confidence and familiarity with what might happen. You can be more effective and less emotional. Copy and practice with the questions that follow. These questions will help you prepare your thinking and plan. Use them as you practice for your discussion. Do not wing it.

Remembering from Chapter 4, Fundamental Strategy, you are using these tools to keep you and the other parties thinking intelligently, not letting the discussion go down the slippery, emotional slope. The tools you use will help you manage your thinking, and direct your thinking towards dialogue.

Another observation about using paper, flip charts, or whiteboards as the workspace for this type of conversation, and in larger group situations, I have observed having a neutral third place to look, vs. into each other's faces, breaks eye contact and lowers the emotion level by keeping the parties focused on what's important on the paper.

And you are encouraged to try any tool from either the

larger group (next chapter) or Chapter 9's Collaboration Tool Box in a smaller group.

NOTE: if you think you're moving into a potentially touchy situation regarding the possible emotional reactions of any of the conversation's parties, I do recommend that you consult with you HR, and possible Legal, departments to be sure what you plan to do is in your and the company's best interest.

Tool Use Preparation Worksheet

The following questions are an example of a brainstorming format to help you prepare for a meeting like those described above. Spend the time necessary, preferably a day or two before an important meeting, so you can improve your chances for success.

Notice that you are targeting the behavior by inquiring about the thinking. The tool you select should help you and the other person(s) think more effectively towards your goals.

1. Situation (include type of conflict: perception, value, or need)?

2. What does the conflict looks like (behaviors)?

3. Goals, Measurements of your intervention (what's a win for your intervention)?

4. Thinking (how are they thinking at the beginning and end of this intervention)?

5. Strategy, Process & Tools (choose from Communication Model, AB See, or SMART criteria)

6. Debrief: How did it go? What will you do differently in the real situation? What will you do the same?

6
Larger Group Collaboration Techniques

As introduced in earlier chapters, the primary purpose of the Good Thinking Series of books is to help individuals and teams to improve their performance by guiding their thinking to make better decisions and build better buy-in.

Improved Company Performance

↑

Improved Decisions & Support

↑

Improved Ideas

↑

Improved Thinking

As with the smaller group tools, keep yourself self focused by asking "What decision should I make next to move me towards my goals?"

Decision Making - Experience Review

In my 30 years in industry I have infrequently seen individuals or teams use structured processes to identify preferred alternatives. More often I see groups spending quite a bit of time talking around the table about alternatives, and personal interests and positions. Then the team notices that time is running out and it's time to decide. Someone presents their favorite, someone else another, and then it's time to vote. The vote takes place, modifications may occur, and the team calls it a win when everyone has a decision they can live with.

A paradox: Using the tools, the hard stuff, is easy. Getting people to work together, the soft stuff, is hard.

I Encourage You to Expect More

As the Chapter 4 - Fundamental Strategy introduced, the impact of decisions comes from two components:

- The decision itself preferably selected according to how it fulfills the goals of an initiative, and,

- The support the decision will have from the implementers. The trick here is to catch energy and commitment from the wonderful principle "people support what they help create." Done well, creative process uses structured steps that allow the participants/implementers to both consider and select the alternative.

Team meeting agendas can document the majority of their items as a series of decisions. Meetings can then be thought of as a huddle: Meet to discuss what we've learned since the last meeting about how to direct a decision. Are we ready to decide? Good decision? Good support? Next decision. please.

An attractive version of the meeting format vision is one with no chairs—just a standing table, huddle up, discuss/decide, break...

As I mentioned earlier, my purpose in this and the previous chapter is not to attempt to present a comprehensive collection of all, or even many, of the collaboration techniques available. There are many good resources of techniques and tools. What I do hope to do is to help inspire (or encourage) you to use techniques and tools like those in this and the next chapter.

And again as with the smaller group tools, the most effective way to learn this collaboration approach is to actually use the tools in either a seminar situation or a real work situation. A note about working team size. If I have more than seven in a client situation that is trying to make a decision, I will often break this group up into smaller working teams. The smaller team members then have more air time while fewer people have silent time. If they are working on the same task, I'll have each team develop a flip chart of their work, then ask one to present it to the larger group, ask for discussion and revision, asking the second team "Anything different?" I have done this many times with groups of 100+. Presentations can be shared with thumb drives via PowerPoint or on overhead transparencies.

In a strategic planning session I will often have a group of 15-20 broken up into five person teams and have the group develop four different planning documents simultaneously (a real time saver), then present them to the larger group for discussion, revision, and buy-off.

The tools I will present in this chapter are pretty easy to use once you are familiar with them, and likely to be used occasionally to frequently. They are most often used in groups of five and above, and often used when the decisions to be made that affect the team and the supporting organization.

1. Brainstorming
2. Affinity Diagram

3. Scoreboard

4. Impact ease diagram

5. Force field diagram

6. Interrelationship digraph

7. Prioritization process: scoreboard, brainstorming, multi-vote, decision matrix

8. Work room set up

Author's note: Most of the tools I use I have learned from other sources. If I remember the source, I will cite it. If I invented the tool, I'll mention it. Otherwise a hearty thank you to those of you who first thought of the tool. In my thinking it's a lot like knots, as with ropes and strings. They were probably discovered accidently, and immediately and willingly shared with others.

1. Brainstorming

Merriam-Webster describes brainstorming: "a group problem-solving technique that involves the spontaneous contribution of ideas from all members of the group."

You've been here before. "Let's have some ideas;" "Let's brainstorm." Your workspace for a team should be a conference room with lots of wall space, plenty of markers, flip charts, Post-Its, tape, etc. to let you easily document your conversations and progress.

There are many ways to brainstorm for ideas. One common process has a facilitator/scribe write down ideas as participants call them out. Common ground rules are "no bad ideas," one person at a time, anything goes, etc.

Brainstorming with Post-Its

My preferred process has the participants starting a session sitting at a table,With a Post-It pad and a narrow felt tip marker. Then each participant silently writes down their own ideas one idea per Post-It sheet. Write large enough so people can read each idea from a distance. All participants are writing on their pads at the same time; the room is quiet. This goes on for about five minutes.

Then to debrief the ideas the participants stand in a semicircle at a flip chart and share their ideas with each other. Each person presents and sells their first idea to the group sharing how their idea fulfills the task. Then you repeat this process until all ideas have been presented. One person at a time, one idea at a time. Do not try to pre-sort the Post-Its, just place them up as they are presented.

Remembering that dialogue can describe the kind of conversation that builds a synergistic new and better understanding of an issue, this should be a very chatty session. These conversations also provide an opportunity for additional ideas to be discussed and posted. This should be a real dialogue session, lots of learning, lots of sharing, challenge when necessary

Process

1. Calibrate your team. Talk for a minute or two having people verbally share the kinds of ideas they're likely to put down to make sure people are on the same page.

2. Generate ideas. Write individual ideas on Post-Its. Give each member five minutes alone to work/ write quietly.

3. Present and discuss ideas: Meet at a flip chart stand or flip chart on a wall and present and discuss idea one at a time. Each person presents one of their ideas as it is their turn.

This method of brainstorming, including the Post-Its, the time alone to come up with your own ideas, the one-idea-at-a-time presentation of ideas to me is the key to the success of this method. The Post-Its and the process are a great leveler—letting quiet people come up with their ideas and knowing they have a chance to present and be heard, and the noisy people to take a minute to think before talking, and not being allowed to dominate the conversation.

2. Affinity Diagram

An Affinity Diagram is a sorting tool used to help identify "natural groupings" of data. It's easy to do this after you have completed brainstorming as I just outlined. A helpful observation after brainstorming: you likely do not have 30-40 different ideas, you probably have about six. The Affinity Diagram is merely an opportunity to recognize and consolidate these similar items. This helps you focus on fewer issues. The number of Post-Its in a group may indicate a level of importance.

Process:

1.   Have team members brainstorm an issue, writing each of their ideas on a single Post-It.

2.   Place all of the collected brainstormed idea-sheets on a flip chart so all of them can be read at one time.

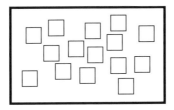

3.   Team members begin to "sort" the cards, repositioning them so they are with other cards similar in idea, into their "natural groupings."

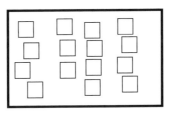

4.   When all of the cards have been sorted into groupings, write a header cards and place them at the top of the groupings.

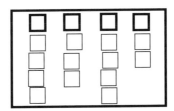

Depending on the group, if there are likely one or two who would direct the process verbally if given a chance, I'll level the playing field and ask the team to complete this part of the exercise silently.

3. Scoreboard

A scoreboard is a document a team develops to describe success for a given initiative. I recommend you use
both Brainstorming and Affinity Diagram to build a scoreboard. Have the team quickly discuss which initiative they
are discussing, in this case the description of a preferred
state; use the five minutes alone to brainstorm with Post-
Its, present the ideas, group them, and title them. The titles are then the components of the scoreboard.

QCDISM is an example, without metrics, used by
manufacturing and many service organizations. It is a
definition of success provided by the American Society of
Quality. It consists of:

- Quality
- Cost.
- Delivery
- Innovation
- Safety
- Morale

If possible the scoreboard will include categories and
numbers. So "improving quality, cost, and delivery" is better than "improve revenues" and "improving quality to 150
DPM, cost to $2.50 per item and delivery to one day" are
even better. The clearer the finish line, the easier it is for
the team to know what they're working towards and to
recognize when they're done.

Example with metrics:

- Quality

- Defects; Six Sigma; less than4 defect per million opportunities.
- Complaints: fewer than 5% customers.
- Rework: costs less than $200,000 per year.
- Cost
  - Operations costs show 4% reduction per year.
  - Warranty costs lowered to less than 2% sales revenues.
- Delivery
  - On-time 99% time.
  - Right product/right place/right time, 90% time.
- Innovation
  - New products: at least five new product in development at any one time.
  - New business: 20% company revenue from products 5 years old or younger.
- Safety
  - Employee accidents occur at Six Sigma or less.
- Morale
  - Employee turnover less than 10% per year.

As a reference point the Scoreboard can be used to help the team see if they are or are not on track. As a dashboard, as in a car, it provides real time data about the important things that need to happen in order for the team to achieve their project's success.

In a hospital emergency room, the scoreboard is the collection of electronic dials and measurement devices that monitor the patient and provide feedback should the patient's condition deteriorate.

Once you know how to brainstorm, develop an affinity diagram, and a scoreboard, improve your brainstorming by developing the scoreboard first. Just what do we want the brainstormed ideas, potential solutions for example, to accomplish? With a scoreboard, the presentation and dicussion of the brainstormed ideas can be compared to the scoreboard. "This idea supports the scoreboard in the following way…"

Extra Credit:

A "Balanced Scorecard" measures both leading and lagging indicators that represent the macro process of a company: develop your employees, make and sell great products and services, treat customers well, and manage your finances. Leading indicators would include: learning and growth, internal business processes, and proactive customer support. Examples of lagging indicators would be financial metrics.

4. Impact Ease Diagram

An Impact Ease Diagram provides a simple flip chart format for a team to place brainstormed options/initiatives (from a brainstorming session) on a grid to identify which they ought to do first (most often: easy to do & high impact).

The process is easy. Have the team brainstorm and post their ideas of how to complete a project on an open flip chart. Format a second flip chart as show below. Then have the team, facing both flip charts, pull one idea from the collection and nominate where it should be placed on the Impact Ease Diagram.

The team ought to support the placement of option.

Discussion should be supported by data based positions, not just opinions.

Flip Chart Format

High Impact		
Low Impact		
	Hard to Do	Easy to Do

5. Force Field Diagram

Sometimes called a Pro-Con list. An alternative brainstorming format. Use to identify significant forces which are restraining you from reaching your goals. Use to narrow your alternatives, but not to choose a single alternative.

Process:

1. Working with team members or others who know the issue best, write a goal at the top of a flip chart.

2. Brainstorm issues which promote the goal, and place them in the left column. Brainstorm issues which restrain the goal and place them in the right column.

3. If helpful, rank the columns separately by the impact they have on the goal you listed at the top of the sheet.

4. Then assign the top restraining forces to team members to reduce or eliminate.

GOAL: Implement Improvement Capability

PROMOTING FORCES:	RESTRAINING FORCES:
customers demanding it	time
company leaders involved	budget
some suppliers can help	last initiative failed
training resources	morale could be better

6. Best of Both Worlds

1. Assemble two teams with opposing ideas in a room.

2. Prepare a flip chart, horizontal, with a force field diagram for each team.

3. Mark the columns of the A-team force field diagram to the left as Negatives, Positives in the two columns respectively.

4. Mark the columns of the B-team force field diagram to the right as Positives, Negatives in the two columns respectively:

Project A Negatives	Project A Positives

Project B Positives	Project B Negatives

5. Title the two force field diagrams with the titles of the two alternative goals and solutions.

6. Working apart in the same room, but on different walls, fill out the force field diagrams listing positives and negatives for each solution.

7. Have each team review their results with the other team while the charts are on different walls

8. Respecting when given two options the best might be the third, put the two flip charts together, edge to edge, A to the left, B to the right. Now work hard to find another solution that fulfills both positive columns and that both project teams support:

Project A Positives + Project B Positives = New Better Project C

Project A Negatives	Project A Positives	Project B Positives	Project B Negatives

7. Interrelationship Digraph

Use to identify which variable in a situation is the most causative, and is probably the best thing to pursue first.

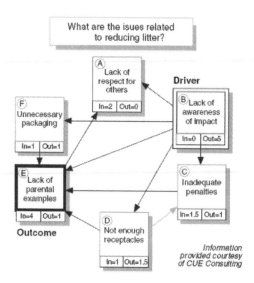

Identify the problem or issue to be addressed.

1. Working with people who know the situation, brainstorm cause-components of the problem. Lack of respect for others, lack of awareness of impact, etc.

2. Arrange causes in a circle on flip chart paper.

3. Draw arrows between all appropriate issue-cards asking, "Which other cards are caused/ influenced by this card?" The arrow points from the source of the cause or influence to the result-card in question.

4.   The most significant cause has the greatest number of arrows coming from it; the best indicator of success has the most arrows going into it.

8. Prioritization Process: Scoreboard, Brainstorming, Multi-Vote, Decision Matrix

One of my favorite sequences of decision making exercises that promotes/provokes dialogue is scoreboard, brainstorm, multi-vote and decision matrix. This may sound complicated but really it's quite easy.

Let's work through an example of trying to select a good car for a five-person family.

Task: Select a good car for a five-person family

Process:

1.   Clarify the task and process. Here let's select a good car for a five-person family.

2.   Have team stand at a blank flip chart sheet. Discuss and document a scoreboard success as measured by:

Example Criteria: (success as measured by...)

• Quality - defects, complaints, rework, etc.

• Cost – operating costs, warranty, etc.

• Practical - good storage space.

• Safety – great crash test score.

• Fun- bells and whistles to include CD, DVD, sporty drive.

3. Generate ideas. Team members document their "ideas" individually on 3" x 3" Post-It's. Write large enough with a felt marker so people can read each idea from a distance.

It is also helpful to calibrate the team by verbally sharing a few of their likely nominations. "Are we on the same page?" It is important to give each member 5 minutes alone to work/write quietly while writing on their Post-Its.

4. Meet at a flip chart stand or flip chart on a wall and present and discuss each idea one at a time. Each person presents one of their ideas as it is their turn. Sell your idea in terms of the scoreboard criteria. Promote dialogue. Dialogue should include people with data clarifying how a particular car does or does not fulfill criteria from the scoreboard. If you weren't sure, you'd suspend the meeting, and go find out. Data drives the dialogue, not opinion.

5. If you end up with more than six options to choose from, quickly narrow the list by having people vote for their favorite options. Give everyone 10 votes but stipulate they can not put any more than 5 votes on any one option. Vote, tabulate, and take the four high scorers to the next step.

6. Select the best choice with the use of a Decision Matrix: using a 5 point impact scale: 5 = great fit, 1 = poor fit. Here you compare each pair/cell. So Choice A, how does it support quality? Team discussion = 4. How does Choice B support quality? Team discussion = 3, and so on.

	Choice A	Choice B	Choice C	Choice D
Quality	4	3	4	5
Cost	2	4	5	3
Practical	4	3	2	3
Safety	4	2	3	4
Fun	5	4	3	2
TOTAL	19	16	17	17

While the four choices are close, if you can agree to support Choice A as the best fit, this collaborative process has helped you make a good decision with good support.

Certainly you would not use a process like this to decide where to go to lunch. But where to build a new facility, probably.

Comparing Collaborative vs Non-Collaborative Approaches

What's different in the above process that this example and approach would be more collaborative (great decision supported by the team) ?

In a simple comparison (we could dig deeper on any example) in a non-collaborative situation it is quite likely the process would look like:

1. Clarify the topic: let's try to list some good cars for 5-person family.

2. Generate ideas. People would begin nominating options verbally at the same time. Or one person might step to a flip chart and list the nominated options.

3. Once all the options were listed, someone would likely say "Let's vote". People move the chart and

place their sticky dot on the car they like best. If one would have the most dots, it would be declared the winner.

Let's consider some of the differences and impact:

Collaborative Approach

- Topic and process clear.
- Team has identified a team set of goals for the selection of a car.
- Team members, given five minutes by themselves, have time to think without the social pressures in teams: performance, being "right", looking good, etc.
- Team presentation of ideas is regulated by the simple "one at a time" rule. This balances participation.
- Team members present their brainstormed option while selling them to the scoreboard helping all the listeners learn how/that a car does/does not fulfill the scoreboard.

Non-Collaborative Approach

- Topic and process somewhat clear.
- Team members are left to consider their own personal set of goals for the selection of a car.
- Team members are encouraged to get right down to work, laying the situation open to many social pressures in teams: performance, being "right", looking good, etc etc.
- Team presentation of ideas is unregulated allowing verbal people to lead the exercise providing unbalanced participation.

- Team members do not compare their brainstormed option with the scoreboard.
- Participants are left with what they knew about cars they like.
- Voting with dots is efficient.

To me the key difference is the shortage of meaningful dialogue in the non collaborative example. The non-collaborative conversation just wanders. One or two people will probably lead the discussion, and the decision. Without the dialogue, there is very little learning, just a competitive series of opinions.

So What?

This, of course, is only one way for a team to select an alternative from a variety of options. The goal in using any technique is to pick an alternative that really supports the initiative's opportunity statement, fulfills the scoreboard, and is developed in such a way that the vast majority of participants and implementers support the final choice. Done well with structured steps, the team is aligned, and excited to implement the idea. Done poorly with aimless conversation, the meeting will be seen as a waste of time.

Large Group Room Set Up Recommendations

Room Set up - Preferred: About 1500 square feet.
(c = chairs)

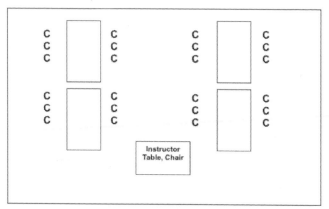

Room Set up - Preferred:

Room has good light (windows to speaker's right and facing wall). Tables set to allow participants to view presenter without having to turn around. Great wall space. A bit crowded.

Room has good light (windows to speaker's left). Tables set to allow participants to view presenter without having to turn around. Great wall space. Great move around space

Room Set up - To be Avoided:

Room has poor lighting (no windows). Tables may require participants to turn around to view presenter. Insufficient wall space.

7
Building a Collaborative Culture: One Big Step

Expanding selective applications of collaboration tools and techniques to a larger organization is like moving into the playoffs of any competitive event. You want to do it in such a way that you get to go on, i.e. you've got to win. Winning requires that you both change the performance of the teams AND that the teams like working the new way.

Warning: Do not ask your employees to be collaborative unless you as their leader are ready yourself. Sort of like asking everyone else to be honest, and you still reserve the right to tell some untruths. It won't work. It may take you months to overcome a careless introduction of collaboration skills.

In this chapter I will recommend one fundamental exercise that has the potential for providing a consistently productive stage for the successful use of collaboration tools and techniques.

To affect a company-wide culture, the results of this exercise would have to affect a process that is used company-wide. I will present a pervasive process that gets cycled frequently, by all the employees, and generates significantly different company performance, and that people would like to do.

The process I will nominate for this focused effort is the process that employees and leaders use to conduct their day-to-day meetings. Appreciate that all the small and large group collaboration tools presented in earlier chapters would most often be used in meetings. I think of meetings as the most frequently cycled business process in the world. As long as decisions have to be made, meetings will be necessary. You cannot eliminate them. Our best option is to make them far more useful, valuable, and say it, fun.

Improve Meetings to Improve Business Performance

Why change meetings? I think changing meetings, so that they can be more collaborative, could be the most important thing an organization could do to improve its performance. If you have decided to move ahead, and develop your organization so it could be more collaborative, improve your meeting process.

This chapter will focus on the place and process where most business decision making takes place - the standard daily decision making meeting process. I will not address all types of meetings or all aspects of meetings. Just face-to-face decision making meetings. This can include creative thinking, generating ideas, brainstorming, analysis, goal setting, problem solving, and above all, decision making.

This chapter will not the be-all or end-all word on how to conduct better meetings. It is a primer to help you think and act in ways that help you develop and conduct better meetings - much better meetings. And to help you decide when and how to continue to improve your meetings as you progressively raise the bar on your expectations about your meetings. Raising the bar will have you selecting and using new and appropriate collaboration tools and techniques.

Business Performance Improvement Requires Better Ideas, Better Thinking

To review from earlier chapters, we will work to develop tools and techniques that guide our thinking for a period of time, to generate better ideas, to support better decisions and behaviors, to improve business performance .

As you've seen in earlier chapters:

Improved Company Performance

↑

Improved Decisions & Support

↑

Improved Ideas

↑

Improved Thinking

Current Reality: The Cost of Ineffective Meetings

Today thousands of companies are spending millions of dollars to help their employees learn to apply Lean and Six Sigma process improvement methodologies to a wide variety of their manufacturing and service processes. Many of these companies claim to be saving many millions of dollars in the doing.

Meanwhile the big offender, how all/most company leaders and employees meet in the millions of meetings every day, begs for help.

The vast majority of decision making worldwide is conducted through meetings. Research estimates that there are 11 million meetings every day in America, or 4 billion meetings a year. Anytime two or more people gather to discuss anything, and often attempt to move towards making decisions, they are meeting. Many meetings are ineffective and inefficient. Many employees resign themselves to "awful meetings". "Hey what are you going to do??? That's just the way it is."

"Too many meetings are poorly run and consume significantly more time than is actually needed to accomplish the necessary tasks. Look at just a few of the statistics:

- According to the Wall Street Journal, CEO's feel that meetings account for the largest share of unproductive time on the job.

- Various studies (e.g., Hofstra University, University of Southern California at Los Angeles) report that attendees say that between 30 and 50 percent of time spent in meetings is a waste.

- Most professionals attend a total of 61.8 meetings per month, each of which last approximately 1 hour.

- An MCI study found that 73% of meeting attendees have brought other work to meetings and 39% say they have dozed during meetings.

- In the same study, meeting attendees admitted that they daydream during meetings (91%), miss entire meetings (96%), or miss parts of meetings (95%)

"With statistics like these it's no surprise that meetings are getting in the way of meeting organizational priorities and achieving its tactical and strategic goals. Meeting attendees are getting frustrated, distracted, and irritable just thinking about having another meeting to attend."

—http://www.effectivemeetings.com

Considerations

"Bad meetings exact toll on the human beings who must endure them, and this goes far beyond mere momentary dissatisfaction. Bad meetings, and what they indicate and provoke in an organization generate real human suffering in the form of anger, lethargy, and cynicism.

"And while this certainly has a profound impact on organizational life, it also impacts people's self-esteem, their families, and their outlook on life.

"The best news of all: for those organizations that can make the leap from painful meetings to productive ones, the rewards are enormous. Higher morale, faster and better decisions, and inevitably, greater results."

—Patrick Lencioni, *Death by Meeting*

Economic Impact – Estimate Your Team's Current Meeting Process Waste

Remember back a few chapters considering that many organizations are spending 10-30% or their revenues generating waste.

You are welcome to contact me at *www.johncanfield.com* to request a free interactive Excel spreadsheet to assist you in calculating the dollar cost of inefficient/ineffective meetings in your organization.

Table 1. Costs of a meeting per employee		
Average hourly pay per employee at meetings	$35	
Benefits (%)	1.3	
Hourly cost of employee attending meeting		$46
Table 2. Costs of company-wide meetings		
Number of employees attending meetings	60	
Number of meetings per day (avg/employee)	3	
Number of meetings per week (avg/employee)	15	
Average Meeting length (hours/employee)	0.5	
Weekly cost of company wide meetings		$20,475
Yearly cost of company wide meetings		$1,023,75
Table 3. Costs of inefficient, ineffective company-wide meetings		
Estimated meeting efficiency and effectiveness (%)	0.8	
Estimated yearly cost of inefficient, ineffective meetings ($)		$204,750
Estimated yearly cost of inefficient, ineffective meetings (employee hours)		4,500
Estimated yearly cost of inefficient, ineffective meetings (# employees)		2.2
Table 4. Better Meetings Initiative - Projected Returns		
Company annual revenues	$20,000,000	
Meeting waste/annual revenues (%)		1.02%
Estimated Cost/employee to address *	$500	
Estimated Cost for company to address	$30,000	
Potential ROI for company to address		682.50%
* = includes both external and internal training and support		
Table 5. Additional costs to be considered and added if applicable:		
Facilities		
Supplies		
Travel, meals, lodging		
Compromised decisions		
Poorly supported decisions		
Unrealized opportunity revenues		

Better Meetings - Improvement Strategy

One thing we have learned since 1980 is that the result in any situation is the consequence of the contributing processes. Strong results are the consequence of strong processes. The converse is also true.

> *"Brilliant process management is our strategy. We get brilliant results from average people managing brilliant processes. We observe that our competitors often get average (or worse) results from brilliant people managing broken processes."*

– Mr. Cho, Vice Chairman of Toyota

Think of meetings as decision-making factories. Work for no defects. Good decision-making meetings actively promote identifying and prioritizing the best choices, while building support for the decisions. Effective processes and their flow charts build in feedback loops upstream and downstream: downstream to confirm you've generated what you intended, and (more importantly) upstream to confirm you're doing what you need to do succeed with the downstream feedback loops. These feedback loops are really questions, represented below with diamond shaped process steps.

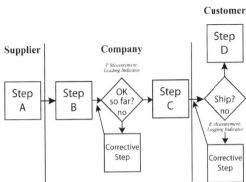

Remember back to an earlier comparison suggesting there are three kinds of decisions and behaviors?

- Intelligent
- Emotional
- Instinctive

When people are stressed they most often default to emotion or instinctive behaviors and often make decisions they later regret.

Using effective thinking processes, like great meeting processes, help keep people thinking more intelligently.

Promote Dialogue & Collaboration - Build Decisions That Teams Support

The goal for an effective and efficient team is to collaborate.

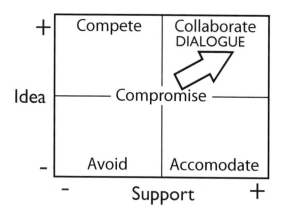

Team Exercise: Build an Effective Meeting Process

Establish a Starting Point: discuss your team's current reality about its meetings.

Use Brainstorming and Affinity Diagram processes to identify, discuss, and prioritize the issues you see slowing your team's meetings. This flip chart then represents your targets. In the next exercise you can build a meeting process that works to prevent these issues from occurring.

EXERCISE
Build Your Meeting Process

1. With the previous exercise (brainstorm and affinity diagram), you have listed what you don't like about your meetings. Identify your 3-5 biggest issues from your affinity diagram.
2. Using Post-Its, silently brainstorm the positive characteristics and steps of great meetings that would help you prevent your list of issues.
3. Write "Meeting Process" at the top left of a flip chart, and "Meeting Ground Rules" at the top right of the flip chart.
4. Using the brainstormed ideas, build a process flow chart on the Meeting Process flip chart along the left side, top to bottom, with those that show sequence.
5. List those ideas that do not show sequence under the Meeting Ground rules heading.
6. Do include any new ideas as they occur to you in your discussion as you work through this exercise.
7. Review your meeting process and ground rules. Will this process and these rules prevent your issues?
8. Add to the bottom of the flip chart an area titled "Team Assessment Criteria" and list how you can build "self control" into your meetings.

   Examples might include:
   a) Are we (am I) following the meeting process?
   b) Are we (am I) following the ground rules?
   c) Did we achieve (are we achieving) the goals of our meeting?

Exercise Follow Ups:

- Do benchmark other team's processes, ground rules, and team assessment criteria. Do they have any ideas you'd like to include in yours?

- Build and begin to use this process with a small group which meets regularly.

- When you are dissatisfied with your meetings over a period of time, modify the process.

Example Meeting Process, Ground Rules, Criteria

PROCESS

A. PREPARATION

1. Have right supplies
2. Invite the right people
3. Schedule the right room
4. Distribute agenda within 48 hours after meeting
5. Schedule scribe, facilitator, and time keeper

B. START THE MEETING

1. Start on time
2. Take attendance
3. Enforce late penalty
4. Review agenda
5. Clarify goals and decisions to be made
6. Explain process/tools to be used
7. Set time limits by agenda item

C. BODY OF THE MEETING

1. Everyone listens
2. Everyone contributes
3. Use tools for problem solving
4. Keep action item list for assignments
5. Summarize Discussions

D. END OF THE MEETING

1. Schedule next meeting if necessary
2. Complete agenda for next meeting
3. Evaluate meeting

GROUND RULES

1. Start on time, be on time
2. No interruptions
3. One meeting at a time
4. No rambling
5. Schedule breaks

MEETING ASSESSMENT CRITERIA

1. Are we following the meeting process?
2. Are we following the meeting ground rules?
3. Are we achieving the meeting goals
4. What will help us to have bett meetings

adapted from "Running Effective Meetings" workshop, Joiner Associates, (now *Orielinc.com*.)

Using Your Meeting Process & Room Set Up

The best way to make good use of your meeting process is to use it religiously for at least four weeks - four meetings if you meet once a week.

I recommend that you identify the roles you need at your meeting (meeting leader, flip-chart scribe, note taker, etc) and develop a matrix like a mileage chart that by lottery assigns these roles for each meeting. a project leader role would not change. Don't settle for waiting for people to volunteer. Everybody helps when their time comes.

Post the meeting process up on the wall and keep standing and pointing to the appropriate process step whenever the meeting is ready to move on or the meeting stalls. Use it just like you use a map as you hike.

Improve your Meeting Process by developing ground rules that address the behaviors of the attending people, not generic.

Start a meeting by reviewing the Meeting Process, Ground Rules, and Assessment Criteria. Ask and post, "What decisions are we meeting to make?"

Maintain your meeting by using the posted Meeting Process, with Ground Rules, and Assessment Criteria as the standard for the behavior you expect from each other. Call each other on any transgressions - don't wait for any meeting police officer - provide the feedback to each other as it provides value - right as it's happening.

As you end a meeting, consider who needs to know whatever was decided during the meeting. Complete the next agenda at the end of the current meeting.

8
Collaboration Tool Box

Collaboration is a primary strategy to help improve company performance.

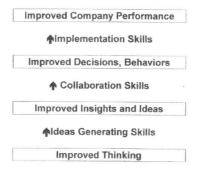

Productive collaboration requires dialogue to help build both an effective decision and cooperative support.

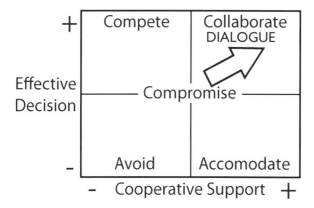

Collaboration tools work because they:

a. Guide a person or team's thinking to develop dialogue to minimize the unhelpful behaviors (avoid, accommodate, compromise, and compete), engaging helpful behaviors (collaborate).

b. Focus on building a great decision using the best ideas, minimizing unnecessary personality friction.

c. Are very interactive and hands on to help build buy-in (people support what they help create).

"Collaboration is the process of shared creation—two or more individuals with complementary skills interacting to create a shared understanding that none had previously possessed or could have come to on their own."

—Michael Schrage, Research Fellow at the MIT, author of two critically-acclaimed books on collaboration

"If you want to teach people a new way of thinking, don't bother trying to teach them. Instead, give them a tool, the use of which will lead to new ways of thinking."

—Buckminster Fuller, American engineer, author, designer, inventor, and futurist.

The following pages will provide introductions to a variety of tools I have found useful in helping teams collaborate. In each case you can learn more from the many resources found on the internet by just listing the tool title in the search field.

There are many resources on the internet to help you learn more about these tools. For example Google web, images, and video.

ANDON CUPS

A possible worldwide first: Meeting andon signals

Think of a meeting as a decision-making factory. You

want your meetings to have no defects and no waste.

You may have heard of andon signals as an integral tool on a lean manufacturing floor, a simple light arrangement to provide feedback about a machine's current state—often in the customary traffic light arrangement: red, yellow, green.

These are operator driven, so if and when the employee finds a problem *they* change the light's status to alert the machine maintenance team to help immediately.

So why not use this in a meeting? I tried this first with a planning team who was working on a series of issues about which there was some strong opinions and disagreement.

I started the meeting as its facilitator, explaining the role of andon board on their manufacturing floor and then brought out my andon devices: simple colored plastic cups, stacked with green on top to start.

I explained how the colors worked to indicate their current level of support for the decision at hand, and encouraged them to keep themselves and me informed of their position on a real-time basis by changing the top cup as they saw fit.

We began the meeting, and clickety-click, the top cups changed colors and we were off. As the meeting progressed the cups changed to green, then to yellow, then back to green and so on. No red cups, to my surprise.

The trick here is to provide an impersonal way for people to express their personal opinions. It may sound silly, but it does work.

I like to challenge the meeting participants to get themselves to a green cup. Influence the team with data to help you end up with a group decisions that you support.

Searching for and finding more helpful ways to think about how teams conduct their business can provide substantial benefits to the team members and their organizations.

BENCHMARKING

Benchmarking, in a business sense, is about comparing your own organization to "the best". How do you measure up compared to the winners?

While wanting to differentiate my organization, and not just "be as good as", benchmarking is also a method to help improvement and innovation teams to" discover what's possible".

With the helpful mental model of a process flow chart, later in this chapter, you are on a treasure hunt for more efficient and effective process flow chart steps and leading indicators.

PROCESS:

It is best to do this work with a team that knows their own processes well, is willing to learn from other process owners, in and out of their company, and likes developing the output to this process up on a wall with lots of flip-charts and Post-Its.

1. **Identify macro-processes key to success.**
   Build a macro flow chart of your company.

2. **Analyze and prioritize key macro-processes.**
   Select the processes which improved would pro-vide the greatest impact to your organization as measured by your Scoreboard.

3. **Identify key micro-processes**.
   Build micro flow charts of the processes selected in step 2.

4. **Identify key metrics for each micro process**.
   Identify and document key P/R measurements (leading, lagging indicators)

5. **Identify potential sources of information.**
   What other organizations in and out of your indus-try might exercise a process you're studying much better that you? Who can possibly show you "what's possible"?

6. **Determine how benchmarks will be col-lected**.
   Plan your treasure hunt by securing or building flowcharts of the process you will investigate. List

your questions before you go. Make arrangements to tour with people who really know the process.

7. **Collect the data**.
Use appropriate means to capture what you see: flow charts, run charts, histograms, procedures, videos, testimonials, etc.

8. **Analyze the data.**

9. **Establish improvement goals and action plans.**

10. **PDCA on process changes.**
Treat data as you would using your organization's Improvement Process.

11. **Incorporate benchmarking into planning.**
Proactively feed your strategic and tactical planning by selecting tasks in reference to company Scoreboards, industry benchmarks, etc.

12. **Keep looking over your shoulder.**
Be open to learning about improvements wherever you may be.

—Adapted from <u>American Samurai</u>, William Lareau

Please see the *Good Thinking Series: Imagine* to learn more about this tool.

BIG PICTURE

This sequence of steps is a great way to build shared understanding of an improvement or innovation team's starting point.

PROCESS:

1. State the goal:

Improve the output of our candy making process.

2. Develop a Scoreboard to measure success for your opportunity statement.

Increase candy pieces/hour to 4,000; maintain machine costs and safety; reduce process cost by 10%

3. This step gives the sequence its name. On a flipchart or two document the situation as part of a system. As a team draw a detailed diagram of the problem and the area that surrounds it. Lots of details about the components and the relationships between the components.

In this step you want to emphasize the goal of this step is to document current reality, not preferred state.
There are a number of models in this chapter that can assist:

a. Relationship Diagram: show how the respective individuals/departments work in a matrix of relationships.

b. Process Flow Chart: this document will show the sequence of the steps to complete.

c. Thinking and Performance. This will use a brainstorming format to allow participants to differentiate helpful and not-helpful thinking and behaviors.

d. Value Chain shows columns of respective vertical processes allowing for appropriate connections between the processes.

e. Workflow Diagram shows how people are moving around in the work area.

4. Discuss the ways in which each component affects the system and the situation's goals. This step's purpose is to

feed a deep dialogue about the opportunity and anything and everything that might be related to the opportunity.

One helpful addition is to use red colored markers to identify components on your drawing that are opposing your goals, and green for components that are supporting your goals.

5. Teams most often follow this sequence with the prioritization sequence presented in chapter six.

Please see the *Good Thinking Series: Imagine* to learn more about this tool.

BUSINESS ENVIRONMENT ANALYSIS

This tool allows a team to objectively describe the "playing field; even and uneven" that their business plays on. I prefer to develop four groups:

1. internal promoting
2. external promoting
3. internal restraining
4. external restraining

While similar to a SWOT analysis (strengths, weaknesses, opportunities, threats) I find the foursome above is more comprehensive – a wider range of topics and forces is discussed.

The types of issues and forces can come from, but not limited to, the following checklist:

- competition
- economic
- environment

- future trends
- governmental
- markets
- political
- society
- technology

Example

1. internal promoting:
   - strong staff
   - firm commitment
   - helpful partners
   - talent pool

2. internal promoting:
   - limited competition
   - market interest
   - client loyalty

3. internal restraining
   - billable hours
   - diverse agendas

4. external restraining
   - employment rate
   - e business buzz
   - dispersion of clients

End the exercise by prioritizing each group to identify the highest impact factors.

Then, as you write your goals with for example SMARTR criteria or strategic planning objectives and strategies, use the data from this tool as a reference. Each goal as written must be able to survive in the business environment listed, taking full advantage of the promoting forces, and minimizing the effects of the restraining forces

Please see the *Good Thinking Series*: *Plan* to learn

more about this tool.

CAUSE AND EFFECT DIAGRAM

Also called a fishbone for its appearance, and an Ishikawa Diagram for its originator.

This tool is primarily a brainstorming format to assist a team in documenting possible root causes.

PROCESS:

Volunteer to be the scribe who will enter team member ideas onto a flip chart sheet in the format listed below which everyone can see.

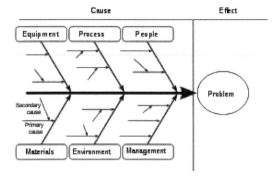

This is a free-flowing, open exercise where team members share their ideas. The fish-bone titles (equipment, process etc) are included on the chart before the brainstorming to focus the team on the most common sources of problem's causes. You can also use your own.

Starting with one bone, equipment for example, what are possible equipment-related causes to our current problem? As this first-level cause is written on one of the lines directly off the bone, you can then ask, "What contributes to this cause?" and write this idea off the first-level line as a second-level cause.

One version of this sequence is called the Five Why's. Ask why five times as you move through the sequence from a first-level cause all the way to a fifth-level cause.

Example - Problem: Plane late to depart

Brainstorming on the "equipment" bone

- **Level 1:** Why is the plane late to depart? Maintenance need.
- **Level 2:** Why is there a maintenance need? Light went off on the cockpit dashboard.
- **Level 3:** Why did the light go off on the cockpit dashboard? Dashboard switch not operating correctly.
- **Level 4:** Why is the dashboard switch not operating correctly? Pilots often put their data binders on the dashboard while they're preparing for a flight breaking the switch levers.
- **Level 5:** Why do pilots often put their data binders on the dashboard while they're preparing for a flight? Binders are too large and heavy, and there is little space to place elsewhere.

This team would be encouraged then to move the pilot data to another provided surface or a small electronic device to eliminate the switch damage.

The purpose of the tool is to sequence great questions that answered with data by the team help the team to discover what is, and what is not, contributing to a problem. Just because an item gets listed on the diagram does not mean it is actually a contributing cause. Resulting causes should be prioritized by likely impact and possibility, and pursued with further investigation.

Please see the *Good Thinking Series: Imagine* to learn more about this tool.

CHARTER

A charter lists expectations within a team and/or between an team and their sponsor. The format of the charter fundamental provides a sequence of very useful questions.

A charter can help:

- An improvement or innovation team   sponsor to think through their request to improve the chances of the impact of the assignment, or
- The team leader to negotiate accountability for the assignment, or
- The sponsor/team leader pair to have a reference for their shared assignment.

Each player (sponsor, team leader, and team members) should work hard to support this completed document before work begins.

DOCUMENT FORMAT:

TEAM CHARTER - SPONSOR PORTION

Project Title:

Project Team Leader Name:

Objective: The end goal for this specific team.(Where are we going?) Objectives should be quantifiable (e.g. reduce scrap, increase productivity) and should be expressed in metrics with actual numbers.

Why Is This Important: Explain how the objective evidence supports the organization's business goals.

Team Members & Skills: Combination of team members to support the project, the skills needed, and any additional resources needed.

Boundary Conditions: Include expectations for the project--what you can and cannot do. Boundary conditions may include limitations (i.e. need more manpower, or more overtime).

TEAM CHARTER - TEAM PORTION

Deliverables: Tangible evidence of work done in support of team objective. Deliverables should be decided upon by the team, and due dates shown on work plan.

Metrics: Quantifiable measurement (trend chart) directly related to objective, showing level of success.

Current Condition: Establish current condition at beginning of project specific to metric.

Target Condition: Desired state of metric upon completion of project.

Ground Rules. Ground Rules include information on how the team will work together, when and where to meet, how does the team handle disputes.

Estimated Completion Date:

Considerations: I prefer that Sponsor Portion is developed together with the project sponsor and the project team leader, and the Team Portion by the whole team

Please see the Good Thinking Series – Imagine to learn more about this tool.

CREATIVE THINKING SKILLS

Truly new ideas often don't often result from "normal brainstorming". It often seems that truly new ideas come from the "accidental" crossing of paradigms, mixing new ideas that just don't logically belong together.

The self organizing capacity of our brains goes to work on this new, unique combination and tries tirelessly to "make sense" of the novel combination. "Lots of ideas" is the wonderful by product. 90% will be thrown away, but 10% will often include ideas, never before conceived, which warrant further consideration.

Example Technique - Imaginary Brainstorming

1. Define the goal or problem: How can we improve sales on the xyz product.

2. Define the essential elements of the problem or goal statement: subject, verb, object. (we, improve, sales)

3. Propose imaginary replacements for one of the elements of the problem statement. It is easiest to start with the subject. One helpful characteristic of

the subject is that it has to be able to think, to have a point of view. Wilder is better; wilder takes you to a stepping stone that you have not exercised before. Select by number of laughs.

4. Formulate a new problem statement, substituting one of the imaginary elements. After you get good at substituting subjects, then try objects, then both. How can aliens improve our sales...

5. Brainstorm the new subject's solutions. Be sure to listen to your imagination and record what it offers you.

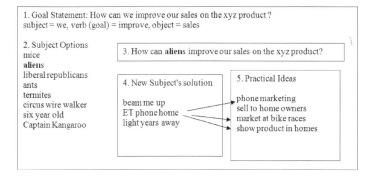

1. Goal Statement: How can we improve our sales on the xyz product?
subject = we, verb (goal) = improve, object = sales

2. Subject Options
mice
aliens
liberal republicans
ants
termites
circus wire walker
six year old
Captain Kangaroo

3. How can **aliens** improve our sales on the xyz product?

4. New Subject's solution
beam me up
ET phone home
light years away

5. Practical Ideas
phone marketing
sell to home owners
market at bike races
show product in homes

6. And now to make it practical. Apply ideas from the imaginary brainstorming back to the real problem statement. How can one of the alien's recommendations help you consider a new practical solution?

7. Analyze all of the brainstormed ideas (real, imaginary, combined) and further explore the more interesting ones.

I define creative thinking skills as the deliberate ability to generate new useful ideas. So these unusual techniques may not generate a 10 million dollar idea every time, but the ideas from these techniques likely did not appear on the first rounds of "normal brainstorming".

COLLABORATE

Please see the *Good Thinking Series: Imagine* to learn more about this tool.

CROSS-FUNCTIONAL PROCESS MAP

This tool's format clarifies cross-functional responsibilities of a process flow chart.

This tool can clarify how functions in an organization complete their work together. This tool shows relationships and sequence. The relationship diagram shows interdependencies.

PROCESS:

1. Assemble the people who most often do the work, at their place of work. Be prepared to gather data in the work place to document the process.

2. Identify the audience you are preparing the process flow chart for. How much detail do they need; macro (big fundamental steps), mini, (smaller fundamental steps), and micro (a level of detail which allows you to document root causes).

3. Complete the macro level flow chart.

4. Identify which functions complete which steps. (bank manager, word processing, etc)

5. List functions on the y-axis of a matrix, with time-sequence along the x-axis.

6. Position process steps in the appropriate row and identify the sequence of steps with arrows.

EXAMPLE - LOAN PROCESS

This diagram shows both the macro level process flow chart above the dark horizontal line, and the cross functional process map below.

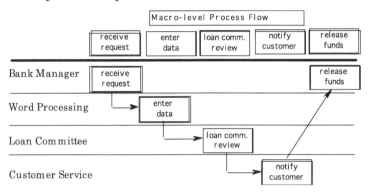

The first benefit comes from using this format to document current reality. How is the process really being conducted? Walk it through right in the workplace to confirm.

Then on another chart identify your preferred routing.

Doing this with either a white board or flipchart and Post-Its allows flexibility as you learn how things are, and how you'd like them to be.

Please see the *Good Thinking Series: Imagine* to learn more about this tool.

CUSTOMER RESEARCH

Successful business depends on the regular transfer of value from one company to another – from the provider to the customer. Knowing what your customer wants and will want is crucial to your success.

Establish and use a process to learn the "voice of the customer". This is one way to gather your customers' feedback. There are many sources and organizations who can help you dig deeper to help you learn what your customers would really like to see from your organization.

Serious customer research can include professional organizations able to solicit analyze statistically valid customer data.

PROCESS:

1. Prepare yourself for a "people to people" process. Study your customers history, their interests, and their company culture.

2. Document the combined process that you and the customer share – your process and theirs (with a value chain for example). Appreciate that your process is upstream from theirs, and that your customer uses the outputs of your process. On this flow chart clarify your process's inputs and outputs, and the customer's process's inputs(your outputs) and their outputs.

3. Prepare and list the questions you will ask the customer to gain insights into the combined process and what the customer likes and dislikes about both your produce and your service.

4. Choose the method you will use to collect data. Options include:

   - surveys: phone, face-to-face, internet survey tools
   - focus groups
   - on-line research
   - user groups
   - voice mail

Regardless of which method you use to collect a larger body of data, do visit a representative group of customers to confirm the data you collected.

5. Before you visit with the customer, practice your questions and interviewing process. It's best to discover what you like to do differently in a practice session with your own teammates, and not in front of the customer.

6. I recommend interviewers visit with the customer in pairs.

7. Meet with the customer at their facility. After introductions walk their process to see how your product/service is actually used by the customer.

8. Ask your questions and record your data.

9. Confirm your understanding of what you learned during the visit with a review of your data with your customer host.

10. Send a thank-you note and provide them a copy of your visit results.

11. Use what you learned from a number of customers to improve the processes that support your products and services.

FLOWCHART BINGO

The purpose of this tool is to assist an individual or a team to wonder aloud about why a particular process is not performing as well as it might.

First: Document a currently troublesome process

Working alone or with a team:

1. Choose a troublesome issue or task that you are currently working on in your organization.

2. Using Post-Its to allow for corrections and flexibility, build a process flowchart for this target process.

3. Remember, this problem is a current natural consequence of a process in place. You may start by first posting the problem as the last step of the process, and post the preceding steps one at a time moving upstream.

4. Remember to include in your flowchart the processes of current P/R measurements; these feedback steps occur early (P = preventative) or at the end (R = result). These steps are posted diagonally to represent questions of "are we OK to this point?" See P/R Measurements in this chapter.

Note: It is important to document your troublesome process as it is, not as you'd like it to be. It is important to challenge someone's perception of how a process is happening. In the best case scenario the listener will not take the challenge personally; they will say, "That's how I see it. Let me show you." And the exercise party heads out to where the process is occurring and sees for themselves what's really happening.

Second: Document the flowchart's scoreboard

See Scoreboard in chapter six.

Third: Flow chart bingo procedures

Dialogue is a conversation that generates learning. Flow chart bingo is a dialogue technique that helps to discover which potential problems are located in which segments of a process.

1. Post your troublesome process flow chart on a wall so all team members can see it easily, or on a table in front of you if you are working alone.

2. Confirm that the flow chart represents the process as it currently operates. Correct if necessary.

3. Using colored dots, create a legend with your flow-chart's scoreboard that lists its preferred performance. Example: Red = quality, green = cost, yellow = delivery, etc.

4. Review your flowchart; compare each process step with each category of your scoreboard.

5. Place a colored dot wherever you believe a major problem occurs.

6. You will create a map of your process's waste targets.

The finished flowchart with a few concentrations of dots becomes a treasure map. Reducing or eliminating the issues highlighted by the dots represents eliminating waste. Eliminating waste is a spectacular money saver.

The history of quality improvement is based on the sequence of these steps: what process is causing the disappointment, what is the standard, what is the gap. Eliminate the gap and pursue the next troublesome process.

Please see the *Good Thinking Series*: *Imagine* to learn more about this tool.

FUTURE SEARCH

Future search is a planning meeting process that helps people transform their capability for action very quickly. The meeting is task-focused. It brings together 60 to 80 people in one room or hundreds in parallel rooms.

Future search brings people from all walks of life into the same conversation - those with resources, expertise, formal authority and need. They meet for 16 hours spread across three days. People tell stories about their past, present and desired future. Through dialogue they discover their common ground. Only then do they make concrete action plans.

The meeting design comes from theories and principles tested in many cultures for the past 50 years. It relies on mutual learning among stakeholders as a catalyst for voluntary action and follow-up. People devise new forms of cooperation that continue for months or years.

Broad Applications

Future search can be used to:

- Create a shared vision and practical action plans among diverse parties.
- Devise a plan and gain commitment to implement a vision or strategy that already exists.
- Initiate rapid action on complex issues where no co-ordinating structure or shared vision exists

People have applied future search in every sector in many cultures. Examples include affordable housing in Santa Cruz, CA, economic development among the Inuit people of North America, AIDS in Bangladesh, more effective business planning in Brazil, business mergers in Germany, sustainable communities in England, strengthening democratic practices in South Africa, regional planning in Indonesia, and education reform across the United States.

Basic Principles and Techniques

Four key principles underlie the future search design:

- Getting the "whole system" in the room.
- Exploring the same global context ("whole elephant") as a backdrop for local action.
- Focusing on the future and common ground rather than conflicts and problems.
- Inviting self-management and personal responsibility for action during and after the conference.

These principles, rather than any techniques, account for the widespread success of future search. You will learn in depth how they function to help people make better communities and organizations. You also will learn techniques that, taken together, put these principles into action, including self-organizing action groups and the critical interplay between small group tasks and whole conference dialogue.

Future Search Network has hundreds of examples worldwide. Please see *http://www.futuresearch.net/*

John Canfield has been trained to facilitate Future Search sessions by Sandra Janoff and Marvin Weisbord, founders of Future Search.

GANTT CHART

Named after Henry Gantt, (1861-1919) an American mechanical engineer and management consultant. These Gantt charts were employed on major infrastructure projects including the Hoover Dam and Interstate highway system. (Wikipedia)

Use as a project management tool to clarify order and length of a project's assignments. The Gantt Chart highlights sequence of assignments and shows when assignments are serial or parallel.

PROCESS:

With the help of the whole project team

1. List all the assignments and sub-assignments. This is easy and flexible with Post-Its.

2. Identify the required sequence of the assignments and place these steps in subsequent rows.

3. Identify which assignments must happen in series and which can happen in parallel. Two assignments in series shows that the first assignment must be completed before the second assignment can begin. For example on the next page, the team cannot begin to enter the data until they have completed receiving the request. This is shown by the project time lines in the two subsequent rows stop and start at the same time.

4. Two assignments in parallel, at least to some degree, shows that a following step can be initiated before you complete the previous assignment. For example on the next page, the team can begin to review the loan before they complete entering the data. This is shown by the project time lines in the two subsequent rows overlap.

5. Present the assignments in the following manner:

EXAMPLE - LOAN PROCESS SCHEDULE

	Monday	Tuesday	Wednesday	Thursday	Friday
Receive Request	▬				
Enter Data		▬▬▬			
Review Loan			▬▬▬		
Inform Customer					▬▬

I prefer that the project teams uses the Gantt Chart as a dialogue tool, using the format to present, discuss, and place the assignments in the order the team supports, indicating the length of an assignment that the team agrees to, and collectively has the team ending the project assignment "on time".

Like other dialogue tools it's a great place to discuss with data about how long things need to take, and which assignment ought to follow or precede another.

Please see the *Good Thinking Series: Imagine* to learn more about this tool.

GREAT TEAM TRAITS

This is a variation of the affinity diagram described in chapter 6.

Great Team Traits provides a team an opportunity to consider, list, discuss, and prioritize the behaviors a team would prefer to see during its project work.

PROCESS:

AT YOUR TEAM TABLE:

1. Individually and silently brainstorm with Post-Its what your successful team is going to be like.

    What will success look like at the major milestones.

    Describe the journey and the arrival.

2. As with the brainstorming process described in chapter 6, have the team meet at a flipchart and present and discuss each person's ideas, one person at a time presenting one idea at a time. Continue placing and discussing until all the ideas are posted.

3. As a team, create an affinity diagram on a flipchart by sorting the team's Post-Its into "natural categories".

4. Write category headings at the top of each group. I'd recommend here to have the headings include action verbs.

5. Discuss insights about the resulting chart. "Does this chart represent what we as a team want to do?"

You have created a "Great Team Traits" scoreboard for your own team. Use it as a reference point when monitoring and evaluating your team's performance.

For example when it's time to assess a team's progress, direct the team's attention to the Great Team Traits flipchart and ask the team "How are we doing? Suggestions for improvement?"

Teams can also raise the bar. If they think there is an area for improvement, they can add new criteria they want to honor.

This is also a great icebreaker for new teams with the advantage that you are creating a useful tool and not just talking about your favorite color or what day of the week you'd like to be.

IMPROVEMENT PROCESS

The improvement process is an example of a systematic step-by-step method built by an organization's Leadership and Guidance Team for improvement teams to use to solve problems and build better processes.

Each step should include tools to guide the improvement team's learning. Each tool is another question. The sum of the answers should lead the team to identify the root cause of a problem and assist their efforts to build an improved process ready to be tested.

There are many variations available to benchmark. Automotive has what they call the 8 D's. Many companies learn the Kepner Tregoe method. A consistent framework for all these methods is the four groups of steps: plan, do, check, act.

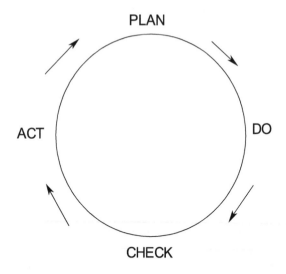

These modern methods following the four major steps are often attributed to either Deming or Shewhart. Others suggest the framework comes from 18th century experimental methodology.

In any case, having the steps with the tools to follow, and the discipline to complete each tool seem to work very well. Modern versions include Six Sigma and Lean methodologies. Using similar methods to target waste and defects saves companies millions of dollars.

EXAMPLE:

PLAN: identify your intended target

1. Establish Team
2. Define Problem Schedule Work
3. Describe Current Situation, Gather Data
4. Analyze, Prioritize Causes
5. Modify Flow Chart

DO: practice to generate feedback

6. Try Out Improvements

CHECK: compare feedback to target

7. Study Results

ACT: implement improvement and create next plan, or revise plan and start again

8. Standardize Improvements

PLAN: identify your intended target

9. Plan Next Improvements

10. CELEBRATE

Please see the *Good Thinking Series: Imagine* to learn more about this tool.

KANO MODEL

The Kano model can be used as a brainstorming format to help a team identify customer expectations, wants, and pleasant surprises.

The purpose of the tool is to differentiate product and service offerings. Done well it requires benchmarking and research to support the tool's brainstorming with data, not just opinions.

PROCESS

The original Kano Model will look like a graph with four quadrants with a diagonal line running from lower left to upper right. This diagonal line emphasizes that the

COLLABORATE

expectations of customers improves over time.

Below the line represents basic attributes. The diagonal line represents performance attributes. The area above the line represents excitement attributes.

> **Basic Attributes** are unspoken but expected. Exclusion of these attributes in the product has the potential to severely impact the success of the product in the marketplace. An example would be any new car buyer expects there to be a spare tire in the trunk. That it's there is no big deal. If it was found missing, especially on a desolate road with a flat tire in the rain, it becomes a very big deal.

> **Performance Attributes** are those for which more is generally better, and will improve customer satisfaction. Conversely, an absent or weak performance attribute reduces customer satisfaction. Of the needs that customers verbalize, most will fall into the category of performance attributes. An example would be the mileage the car can get. Many car buyers are selecting cars based on their mileage. "Our car's mileage is as good or better than our competitors."

> **Excitement Attributes** are unspoken and unexpected by customers but can result in high levels of customer satisfaction, however their absence does not lead to dissatisfaction. Excitement attributes often satisfy latent needs – real needs of which customers are currently unaware. In a competitive marketplace where manufacturers' products provide similar performance, providing excitement attributes that address "unknown needs" can provide a competitive advantage. Although they have followed the typical evolution to a performance

then a threshold attribute, cup holders were initially excitement attributes.

In New Orleans this is called lagniappe and means a little bit extra, like a baker's dozen—thirteen—one extra—free!

You can also use a simple format. On a flipchart, draw lines to create three columns with the following titles: basic attributes, performance attributes, and excitement attributes.

Then have the contributing team brainstorm, discuss, and place their data in the three columns, one column at a time. Lots of discussion, lots of data presentation. Lots of learning.

The overall goal of the exercise is to help the team confirm they are quietly fulfilling the customers' basic attributes, advertising and attracting customers to the performance attributes, and finally, with both the basic and performance attributes fulfilled, then providing something to the customer that pleasantly surprises them, encouraging them to select your product or service.

KEY DECISION CHART

Often when team members are attending a planning meeting, tactical or strategic, they have not prepared themselves to have data driven expectations for the outcome of the meeting.

The Key Decisions Chart is an effective brainstorming format to prepare a meeting leader-attendee to think about their upcoming responsibilities in terms of decisions their team will need to make.

Each leader develops a Key Decisions Chart a few

weeks before the planning session. Their chart outlines their department's key decisions that need to be made within three time periods: Year 1, Years 2-3, and Years 4-5. This can be developed on a flipchart or in an Excel spread sheet.

The sheet has three columns (time periods) and five rows (five key decisions/support). Each of the fifteen cells would list the following information:

1. Topic:
   a. Decision to be made:
   b. Do I have the **data** to make the decision?
   c. Do I have the **support** to implement the decision?

It is also helpful to assign a colored dot alongside the description of each topic's data and support listings to indicate the author's level of comfort with this task.

- green = on track

- yellow = needs some attention, speed bumps present

- red = needs lots of attention, roadblocks present

The meeting to present the Key Decision Charts takes place a few weeks before a planning session. This is a collaborative dialogue session. Each planning team member presents his or her chart to the whole planning team. The yellow and red dots provide some focus for the presentation "Here's where I'm in need regarding a topic/decision/support – who can help me with recommended contacts, approaches, resources, etc ?"

Chart example for one of the cells:

KEY DECISIONS CHART		Name - Date
Year 1	Years 2 - 3	Years 4 - 5

1. Site Consolidation
1a. Should we consolidate the operations currently at sites X and Y?
  ✓ 1b. (data) I need to know the financial implications across all the sites
  ✓ 1c. I need the support of both sites.
	same format as column 1 considering years 2-3	same format as column 1 considering years 4-5

Importantly the purpose of the presentation is not to look good. This is a meeting to help the team recognize where they need to do some work to improve their ability to write a more effective strategic plan. Honest presentation and feedback is crucial.

This chart boils down to being a department's target list for its own functional strategic plan. It's value comes from both the preparation by the functional leader and the valuable dialogue among other functional leaders during the presentations.

Please see the *Good Thinking Series: Plan* to learn more about this tool.

LEADING CHANGE

While leading a major change effort can be daunting, there are a number of resources that can ease the change agent's work and angst.

I first like to appreciate that any change effort is going to irritate some people. Some, many, people dislike change. I find the following a model helpful to consider.

The people you are going to include in your change effort will be in one of the four following corners.

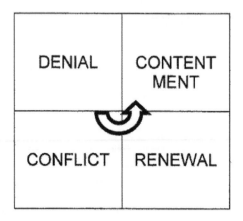

Claes Janssen's talks about the four corners being apartment rooms. The model describes the states of emotion and thinking your audience will be experiencing.

While the goal is to help each person move from denial through conflict and renewal, to contentment. It is important to appreciate that others who are in the other quadrants are there to begin with for their own good reasons.

A productive strategy to move employees is to ask questions, that answered by the employees, help them move into the next quadrant.

I like to combine this model with John Kotter's *Leading Change* series of steps. The book's chapters provide the detail to the questions of these steps:

1. Establish a sense of urgency

2. Create a guiding coalition

3. Develop a Vision & Strategy

4. Communicate the Change Vision

5. Empower broad based action

6. Generate short-term wins

7. Consolidate gains and produce more change - maintain the momentum

8. Anchor the new approaches in the culture

Kotter's steps 1-4 help people move from denial to conflict.

Kotter's steps 5 and 6 help people move from conflict to renewal.

Kotter's steps 7 and 8 help people move from renewal to contentment.

This use of a combination of tools is an example of assembling helpful questions that can guide the learning of a team that wants to improve and engage as many people as possible in the work.

Please see the *Good Thinking Series: Plan* to learn more about this tool.

MOMENTS OF TRUTH

Moments of Truth is a brainstorming format that can help a team identify customer expectations as the experiences your products and services.

The purpose of the tool is provide a format to think about, document, and improve how an organization supports customers.

PROCESS:

1. Assemble the people who know most about your customers' interaction with your product and/or services.

2. Use a process flow chart as a format for your data collection and discussion.

3. Choose the start point and end point of the process you want to focus on.

4. List each process step as the customer would experience them. Represent process steps in boxes and describe with nouns and verbs. Post-Its are a good format for this work.

5. Include under each process step a prioritized list of what the customer wants at each step, and the degree, positive or negative, that you are supporting the customer wants.

   To the purpose of robust dialogue, to find the truth, people should challenge any possible inaccurate assumptions. Try when possible to back up the data in and under the process steps with data, not just opinions or hopes.

The notion of "moments of truth" comes from Richard Normann, who argues that a service company's overall performance is the sum of countless interactions between customers and employees that either help to retain a customer or send him to the competition.

The idea was later used by Jan Carlzon when he was CEO of Scandinavian Airlines back in 1986 and described the idea: "That spark and the emotionally driven behavior that creates it explain how great customer service companies earn trust and loyalty during "moments of truth": those few interactions (for instance, a lost credit card, a canceled flight, a damaged piece of clothing, or investment advice) when customers invest a high amount of emotional energy in the outcome. Superb handling of these moments requires an instinctive frontline response that puts the customer's emotional needs ahead of the company's and the employee's agendas" (adapted from Shep Hyken, *www.hyken.com*).

This tool can help a team build a deep shared understanding of how the customer is experiencing a company's products and services.

P/R MEASUREMENTS; LEADING, LAGGING INDICATORS

Use to this tool to document and clarify the locations and metrics of your process flowchart feedback loops.

Feedback loops are questions within or at the end of a process flow chart that ask if certain conditions are met at that point in the process. If so, move on. If not, the feedback loop should direct the process owner to a corrective step.

Your goal is to identify and implement measurements that allow you to monitor a process while it is operating and prevent process errors.

Here is an example of a flowchart that describes how a product moves from the supplier, through an organization, and to the customer.

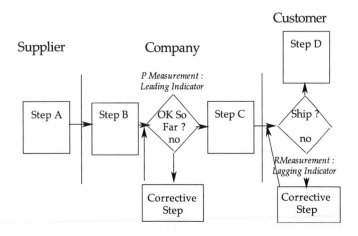

For simplicity I have shown only two feedback loops.

1. After Step B, is the product good so far? No defects? No problems?
2. After Step C, is the product good to ship? No defects? No problems?

In both cases, if the answer is no, the product moves to a corrective step before it can re-enter the process.

Our goal is to provide a defect-free product to the customer. I would prefer to identify any possible problems up stream in my process so I can either prevent the problems, or catch the product from moving on if it is defective. It is helpful to have both P and R measurements.

Feedback loops upstream to prevent problems (P - **p**rocess, **p**reventative, **p**roactive, etc), and downstream (R - result) to confirm the product has no problems and is ready to ship.

An improvement team's goal is to place a sufficient number of P measurements in a process to prevent any possible defects, and assure my preferred results at the R measurement.. A second level of P measurements can help me reduce waste.

Please see the *Good Thinking Series: Imagine* to learn more about this tool.

PARETO DIAGRAM

This tool helps a team identify the significant few, and the trivial many, when wondering which options to pursue – which are important, which are not.

Often called the 80/20 rule. It seems to describe a principle that has you consider that 80% or your problems come from 20% of your customers, 80% or your revenues come from 20% of your customers, etc.

Many examples are available to consider on Google Images.

One way to develop a practical Pareto Diagram is to have a team identify a goal, say problems with a team's performance. Have people brainstorm with Post-Its all the possible causes of poor team performance, move them into an affinity diagram, and then take the groups, from the largest group, to the smallest group, and reposition the Post-Its into a stacked bar graph. With the largest group, start with the lower left of a flipchart, and stack all the Post-Its in a tall column.

Then do the same with the next largest group of Post-Its. Repeat until all the groups are posted.

You have created a Pareto Diagram which shows which cause of poor team performance has the most Post-It entries, and hence the highest bar in the diagram.

You would then be encouraged to target the first column's title to work on first to improve a team's performance.

The Pareto Diagram encourages you to identify and target the short list of to do's, and not distribute your attention randomly across a wider range of alternatives.

PROCESS DECISION PROGRAM CHART

The process decision program chart is a planning tool used to identify and arrange the steps of a project's process steps and sub steps, anticipate the possible problems and consequences of the steps, and consider proactive responses to possible problems. It is a form of scenario thinking.

PROCESS:

1. Gather the team which will be affected by the process.

2. Identify the process and document with a macro process flow chart.

3. Gather 2nd level steps, What If's, and Possible Reactions information and arrange in the following format:

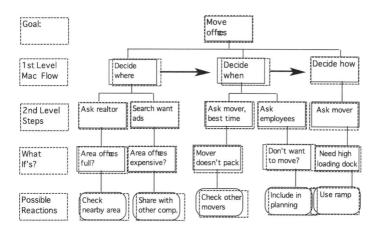

4. Openly nominate and post potential What Ifs (speed bumps and road blocks) for each 2nd level step.

5. Carefully develop possible reactions to the What Ifs.

PROCESS FLOW CHART

The process flow chart may well be the most useful tool for teams to use talk about how things happen, and how they should happen.

Process flow charts are visual maps that show the cause and effect steps and sequence of how work gets done.

Appreciate that the process flow chart format is another way to brainstorm ideas. The accuracy of the flow chart must be confirmed with data.

Process flow charts can be drawn at any level of detail. Here I am showing three levels: macro, mini, and micro.

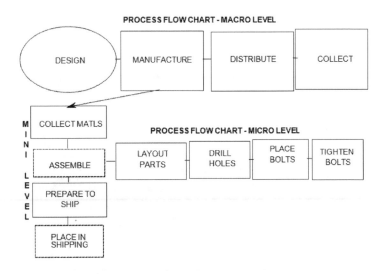

- macro (big fundamental steps),
- mini, (smaller fundamental steps), and
- micro (a level of detail which allows you to document root causes).

When trying to solve problems, work first to identify how the work is actually being done by documenting the process where it's happening, with the people doing the work, and with data from the process.

If you're trying to solve a problem, appreciate that the flow chart you draw, if accurate, describes a process that creates the problem.

EXAMPLE PROCESS

1. Assemble the people who most often do the work, at their place of work. Be prepared to gather data out in the work place to document the process.

2. Identify the audience you are preparing the process flow chart for. How much detail do they need;

3. Choose the start point and end point of the process you want to focus on. Represent process steps in boxes and describe each step with a nouns and verbs.

4. Complete the chart and confirm for accuracy.

5. The conversation that develops this chart should be honest and robust. Using a flip chart and Post-Its allows flexibility for changes and improvements.

Flow charts would be used next to document the preferred sequence of new steps that would generate a better result.

Please see the *Good Thinking Series: Imagine* to learn more about this tool.

RELATIONSHIP DIAGRAM

A relationship diagram helps a team identify the components of an organization's system and the relationships between those components. This tool is often used when teams are beginning or reviewing their macro-level goals. Can be used in conjunction with a cross functional process map to highlight sequence.

PROCESS:

1. Starting with a flip chart, place "function boxes" of company functions (sales, customer service, manufacturing, R&D, etc.) in center of the flip chart. Using Post Is make this flexible.

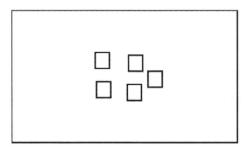

2. Draw a box around the functions that represent the organization

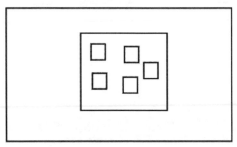

3. Place "function boxes" of company-partner functions (customers, suppliers, delivery, banks, shareholders, etc.) outside the box.

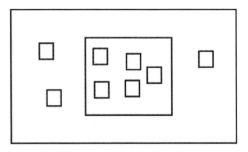

4. Draw <u>and title</u> single-ended arrows between function boxes to identify what value information, or-

ders, money, ideas, capital, etc.) is transferred from whom to whom.

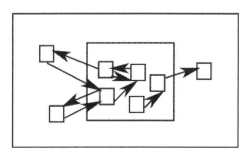

5. Discuss findings with team.

Like many other "current reality" brainstorming tools, the dialogue that helps build this diagram must be open and honest. When done, it's sort of like a circuit diagram. "Where are the shorts?" Where should there be a relationship line and there isn't, or where does the line represent a troubled relationship?

SCENARIO PLANNING

The executive summary of scenario planning might read: Efficient and effective dialogue technique which helps participants generate valuable insights about how a company works within itself, with its customers, suppliers, partners, etc, and how it might deal with a number of possible futures.

The significant benefit of this technique comes from the deep dialogue that the different scenario stories provoke.

The alternate views generate new insights about a company and its future.

EXAMPLE PROCESS

Step 1. Identify Issue and the decision to be made
Best case the question is a yes or no question that the group is struggling to answer.

Example: What kind of car should we build in the coming years?

Step 2. List key factors that affect the above decision
What would you want to know to assist you in answering the question from step 1? Examples: market size, growth, volatility, customers.

Step 3. List driving forces that generate the key factors listed in step 2 (macro) Examples: STEEP: social, technical, environmental, economic, political, predetermined elements that influence key factors, critical uncertainties.

Step 4. Rank the combined listing of items from steps 2 and 3 in terms of impact and uncertainty.

You work to identify two factors.

Step 5. Select scenario logic. In the example below the two factors from step 4 are fuel price and value orientation. Notice how you identify and label the end points of each factor, consider the quadrant and its situation, and title each alternative future (engineers challenge, etc.).

Example: Design Criteria for Entry Level Automobiles

High-Price Fuel

Engineers Challenge
• efficiency
• protectionism

Green Highways
• smaller cars
• versatility

Neo-Traditional
Values

Inner-Directed
Values

Long Live Detroit
• muscle cars
• brand loyalty

Foreign Competition
• sportier cars
• light trucks and vans

Low-Price Fuel

Step 6. Flesh out scenario. Here the team would spend a number of hours describing the future in each quadrant, with a 10-, five- and three-year view for example, as if it has happened.

Step 7. Identify implications of scenarios on decisions Done well, this thinking event generates a wide variety of insights that should be noticed, discussed, and considered against the step 1 question.

Step 8. Select leading indicators, sign posts. A serious team will assign leading indicators to themselves to monitor and report regularly to catch any change in new information that would alert the team a portion of another future is beginning to play out.

Step 9. Answer question listed in #1 above.

Please see the *Good Thinking Series: Plan* to learn more about this tool.

SIX THINKING HATS - Edward de Bono

A great tool to promote dialogue, Six Thinking Hats, developed by Dr. Edward de Bono, provides a practical framework that encourages the exploration of ideas.

In many organizations generating good ideas is a difficult process. When egos, emotions, information, and logic are all mixed together, the thinking process can become limited.

A story often shared in training circles is about five blind people who had never seen an elephant. The five circled the animal and touched it with their hands to gather data. When they shared their findings, the person near the trunk could only describe a long cylindrical object. The one near the feet viewed the elephant as a massive tree trunk. The third, who was at the tail, reported something all together different.

One option for this team would be to argue about their own points of view to confirm their findings and egos. Another would be to accept that, because of their point of view, they were limited in what they could learn from their own vantage point. They could appreciate their fallibility and open the conversation to all points of view, working to integrate these points of view into a single comprehensive understanding of the whole elephant.

Six Thinking Hats does a great job of walking a team around their elephant, around their issue, gathering useful data efficiently, with six points of view, while suspending judgment, promoting team learning, and helping the team to arrive at a shared understanding of an issue before they move toward making a decision.

The trick here is to guide a team's thinking to get ideas on the table while the team suspends judgment. De Bono suggests there are six types of thinking that you unconsciously use every day.

Each metaphorical hat represents one of those six ways of thinking provoked by a question:

• White Hat - What do we know and want to know?

- Black Hat - Why might the idea not work?
- Yellow Hat - Why might the idea work?
- Red Hat - What is your intuition about the idea?
- Green Hat - What are some alternatives to the idea?
- Blue Hat - Knowing what we know now, what should we do next?

Used correctly, the process encourages people to separate fact from opinion, to look fully at both positive and negative opinions and to get hidden agendas that can sabotage any meeting on the table. It stimulates their innate creativity and helps them discover how to turn seemingly insoluble problems into real opportunities.

Used correctly, the hats keep your different kinds of thinking separated, focused and controlled. They enable you to evaluate situations objectively by consciously switching in and out of the six thinking modes (hats). This process teaches an individual to look at decisions and problems systematically.

I have seen few groups who have only "read the book" realize the full benefits of this approach. I encourage you to find an experienced qualified trainer and learn to use the hats correctly.

SPEAKER SCORING

Many meetings include presentations by team members to their larger team (Key Decision Charts for example).

The following process is helpful when team members are presenting to each other. The goal is to build great plans which are by themselves substantive and feasible, and that the plans together are aligned and synergistic.

Each team member should consider the following four criteria when listening to and evaluating a team member's presentation. Our focus is on the substance of the presentation, not the delivery.

A) Would you commit your limited and valuable resources to this plan?

    4 - without a doubt
    3 – with a few reservations (list on your scoring sheet)
    2 – with a number of reservations (list on your scoring sheet)
    1 – no (list your reasons on your scoring sheet)

B) Is the plan comprehensive; how many open issues and questions?

    4 - without a doubt
    3 – with a few open issues and/or questions (list on your scoring sheet)
    2 – with a number of open issues and/or questions (list on your scoring sheet)
    1 – no (list your reasons on your scoring sheet)

C) Does the plan complement the overall objectives and strategies for your whole company?

    4 - without a doubt
    3 – with a few reservations (list on your scoring sheet)
    2 – with a number of reservations (list on your scoring sheet)
    1 – no (list your reasons on your scoring sheet)

D) What is the plan's chance of success? Add up the three scores and compare to:

    12 - 10 = High
    9 –7 = Medium

6 - 0 = low

A plan may require a high commitment of resources, be well thought out, meet the objectives but still carry a high risk of success, thereby giving it a high mark if the risk is mitigated by the potential gains.

Sharing your score with the speaker with the team in attendance is the first step in sharing your point of view and helping the team to engage in a useful dialogue about how this and the other presentation's content can best be coordinated and optimized.

Without a structured, value based process like this to provide each speaker feedback, the presenters will unfortunately be thanked with a polite response (artificial harmony) but be raked over the coals at the water cooler.

This process helps speakers learn how they can more effectively lead with the whole organization.

Please see the *Good Thinking Series: Plan* to learn more about this tool.

STORYBOARD

Disney gets some of the credit for this idea. In days past they used story boards to have a flexible location to put cartoon drawings so reviewers can see how all the pictures fit together.

Storyboards can be use in companies to document an Improvement Team's work as they progress through their improvement process. As a team completes the work of each improvement process step, they either post the actual work, often on flip charts, or a summary review, up on the storyboard.

Best case the storyboard becomes the place where a

project's leadership sponsors can go regularly to see how their team is doing without attending or micromanaging the project team.

STORYBOARD - IMPROVEMENT PROCESS STEPS continues

1	2	3	4	5	6
Establish Team	**Define Problem**	**Describe Current Situation**	**Analyze, Prioritize Causes**	**Modify Flow Chart**	**Try Out Imprvmnts**
•assigned process	•brainstorm	•process flow chart		•process flow chart	•process flow chart
•meeting process	•affinity diagram	•rel diag	•brainstorm	•P/R meas	•checksheet
•impmnt process	•scoreboard	•value chain	•cause/ effect dia	•buyoff #1 meeting notice	•run charts
•leadership buyoff criteria	•Gantt chart	•cross functional process map	•pareto diagram	•etc	•etc
•etc	•etc	•etc	•decision matrix		
			•etc		

STRATEGIC PLANNING

Strategic Planning can be considered a sequence of useful questions that when answered by all members of a senior team documents and clarifies 1) the fundamental reasons for organization's existence, and 2) the sequence and accountability of the tasks necessary to fulfill the mission, principles, vision, and objectives.

Most important here is the deep dialogue among the planning members to build both alignment and synergy.

The Plan then should be used consistently as an operational document serving as a reference in all levels of decisions throughout an organization. Does this new task support the Plan?

Common Plan Components (questions):

1. **Mission:** "who we are, what we do"; ultimate intent of organization; no time constraint.

2. **Principles:** "how we work together"; rules about how we treat ourselves, each other, and our community.

3. **Vision:** "where we want to be"; a long view, 3-5 years, of what must be accomplished to support the Purpose.

4. **Scoreboard:** "success as measured by..."; tactical or strategic; measurable performance expectations.

5. **Business Environment:** "playing field; even and uneven"; listing of internal and external promoting and restraining forces.

6. **Objectives:** "what to do next"; specific milestones of what must be accomplished in the next year to support the Vision. Usually three to five are useful.

7. **Strategies:** "how to" accomplish Objectives while considering business environment requirements. Usually three to five per Objective are useful.

8. **Action Plans:** "to do assignments"; quarterly, prioritized action steps necessary to support the Objectives and Strategies. Usually three to five per Strategy are useful.

9. **Plan Implementation Considerations:** proliferation plans, announcements plan,

budget plan, barriers. Fit with and support to Annual Plan.

10. Plan Monitoring Considerations: criteria and plan to monitor your progress

Think of these documents as a hierarchy of intent, from the biggest ideas all the way down to the entries in your daily planner.

Strategic planning provides a macro multi-year view of where you want to go, and broadly how.

Another planning process, Annual Planning, provides a focused micro single-year view of how you will organize and exercise the resources necessary to achieve your strategic plan and include the following components: Income statement, Balance sheet, Cash-flow analysis, Sales and marketing plan, Capital plan, Inventory plan, Organization charts, and Compensation plan

Please see the *Good Thinking Series: Plan* to learn more about this tool.

SYSTEMATIC DIAGRAM

Also called Tree Diagram, or Dendogram

Another brainstorming format, this tool uses a flip-chart and Post-Its to help a team identify and arrange paths and tasks to achieve primary and supporting goals, or as a cause and effect diagram, effects and different levels of causes.

PROCESS:

1. Complete brainstorming exercise listing all steps required to complete project.

2. Arrange the steps in the following manner:

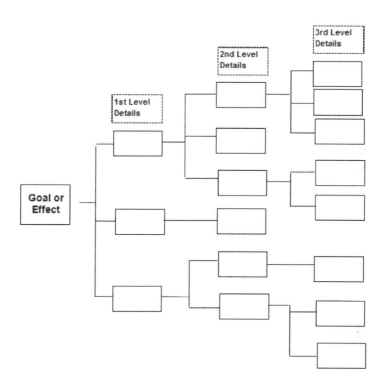

THINKING AND PERFORMANCE

This tool and exercise helps a leadership team develop a culture specific listing of success-promoting and restraining thinking and behaviors. This exercise is based on a General Electric model linking an organization's performance with its' culture.

This is a data driven 180 degree performance review providing an opportunity for direct reports to assess their leaders. This tool's dialogue considers results but focuses on the contributing thinking and behaviors that drive the results.

PROCESS:

Randomly select the sequence of leaders to be evaluated. Work on one leader at a time, completing their chart before moving on.

Identify promoting and restraining behaviors

a. Working first alone and silently identify and list <u>behaviors</u> of the leader on Post-Its, <u>one per sheet</u>, that promote or restrain your success. How does this leader help or hinder you in your job?

b. Working with your own list, pick your top three promoting behaviors, and top three restraining behaviors. Document six behaviors per leader.

c. Begin a discussion with your peers, moving around the table one-person-at-a-time, presenting one behavior per turn.

d. As the presenter discusses the behavior, they explain their view about how this behavior promotes or restrains success at your company. Dialogue, dialogue.

e. Place behavior Post-It on matrix in appropriate quadrant.

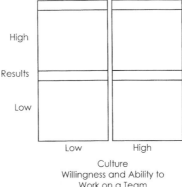

High

Results

Low

Low   High

Culture
Willingness and Ability to
Work on a Team

f. Continue until each person has placed their six behavior Post-Its. Tick mark duplicates to document frequency.

g. Take all promoting behaviors and create an affinity diagram; the category titles will be the parameters for the right side of your culture axis.

h. Take all restraining behaviors and create an affinity diagram; the category titles will be the parameters for the left side of your culture axis. Identify titles for your culture axis

i. Finally, consider the behavior titles and discuss and document the thinking you think that drives those behaviors.

Best facilitated by a person outside the company who can neutrally collate and present the data to the leadership .team members, one-on-one, and then the aggregate to the larger leadership team.

VALUE CHAIN

Teams can use a value chain to brainstorm, confirm, and document how value transfers between company and company-partner groups.

The macro components of a company's system are represented in the chart below:

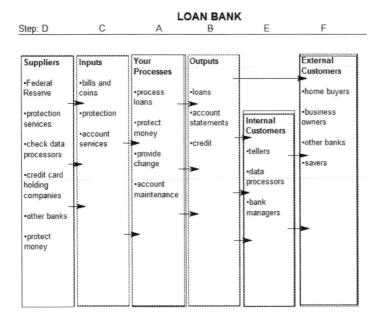

LOAN BANK

Step: D C A B E F

Suppliers	Inputs	Your Processes	Outputs	Internal Customers	External Customers
•Federal Reserve	•bills and coins	•process loans	•loans	•tellers	•home buyers
•protection services	•protection	•protect money	•account statements	•data processors	•business owners
•check data processors	•account services	•provide change	•credit	•bank managers	•other banks
•credit card holding companies		•account maintenance			•savers
•other banks					
•protect money					

From left to right: suppliers, who provide my process's inputs, which my processes use to generate outputs (products and services) for both internal and external customers.

PROCESS:

1. Assemble the people who lead the functional groups and know the most about what their group receives (inputs) and provides (outputs).

2. Outline a system wide (company and company-partner groups) macro-process flow chart like the one just presented.

3. Identify and list the inputs and outputs for each group. Note column-step sequence:

This version has you

- start with your own processes (step A), and then
- ask what outputs (step B) do our processes produce (products and services). Then to
- discuss and capture the   inputs to our processes (step C),   and the suppliers to those outputs (step D). Finally to
- post the customers of the outputs, internal customers (step E) and external customers (step F)

As with other brainstorming formats, you want lots of dialogue and challenge to the many assumptions about how things actually get done in the system you are   discussing.

WASTE SEARCH

Not too many years ago a manufacturer would have an "acceptable scrap" entry in his balance sheet. This pretty much accepted that waste was inevitable, and to keep it pretty low was a noble goal.

COLLABORATE

With the advent of teams using tools like process flow charts and improvement processes to really dig into how processes were really being conducted, many forms of waste have come to our attention.

For a company that cannot deliberately improve their processes, this waste is estimated to be 10-30 percent of the organization's revenues. This waste is often hiding in company processes.

"There are many examples of waste in the workplace, but not all waste is obvious. It often appears in the guise of useful work. We must see beneath the surface and grasp the essence."
—Dr. Alan Robinson,
Modern Approaches to Manufacturing Improvement

One of the most famous searchers of waste was Taichii Ohno of Toyota. A significant contribution of Ohno's was his list of the Seven Sources of Waste:

1. Overproduction—too much of the right products or services; extra work

2. Waiting - delayed action; forgetting

3. Inventory; work-in-process - deteriorating products or services; un-used training

4. Unnecessary processing—too many steps; no added value

5. Transportation—excessive time or distance between stations

6. Motion within work station—in our day-to-day jobs

7. Defects, errors

The key benefit of lists like this is it provides a taxonomy to assist improvement teams in recognizing, understanding, and prioritizing sources of waste.

Another taxonomy useful with service producing processes:

Twelve Cornerstone Tools

1. Bureaucracy elimination : unnecessary administrative tasks

2. Duplication elimination : identical activities

3. Value-added assessment: contributes to customer expectations

4. Simplification : reduce complexity

5. Process cycle-time reduction : shorten cycles

6. Error-proofing : Poka Yoke

7. Upgrading : effective use of capital

8. Simple language : easy for user to comprehend

9. Standardization : selecting a single way

10. Supplier partnerships : improve inputs

11. Big picture improvement : systems view

12. Automation and/or mechanization : free up people from routine tasks

—Dr. H.J. Harrington
Business Process Improvement

9

Implementing and Executing

To be a successful organization, there are only two things you need to do: improve and innovate. Improvement requires removing waste and defects from current processes. Innovation requires building new processes, without waste and defects, that add differentiating value to your customers.

Imagine at this point that you are or want to be a change agent for improvement and innovation in your organization. You want to help your organization become more collaborative in a very deliberate way. To use the tools and techniques to help teams learn and decide efficiently and effectively–not just to assemble people in different formats but with little different support.

This chapter will include a number of considerations and recommendations to encourage and support your work in the coming months and years.

More Change Coming - Are You Prepared?

One thing that will remain the same: change will continue to occur. As it's been said, "The future's not what it used to be." We experience change every day: in business, in our communities, in our homes, in our churches. Often change has a bad rap. We are creatures of comfort and don't mind things staying the same for a while so we can enjoy the good times, enjoy a rest, not have to think about it.

Competitiveness Requires Change

But we live in a competitive world. Commerce is now global and for us to succeed we must be able to compete with, better exceed, our competition in providing products and services to our global markets.

To compete we must improve and innovate. To improve and innovate we must change. To change we must start doing something new, and stop what we have been doing that doesn't help anymore.

One way to think about this has us deliberately substituting "improvement" or "innovation" for "change" at every chance. When we can "operationalize" improvement and innovation (change), when we can improve and innovate first and faster that our competitors, then we are acting proactively to secure our future.

Successful Change Strategies – Characteristics

From earlier chapters, the summary of my change (improvement & innovation) strategy: target the thinking skills.

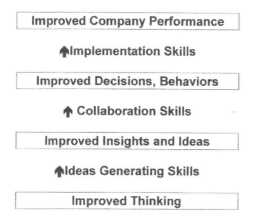

To change our thinking skills is probably easier said than done. What does it take to change a habit? Perhaps you have tried change on a personal basis. Whether it's to read more, weigh less, exercise more, sleep less, many people target personal goals. Thinking back, just how successful have you or a friend been in actually achieving the target?

Successful goal achievers often report a laser beam focus on their goal, a discipline and schedule to the work to achieve it, honest feedback and encouragement, and a celebration of the new process that supports maintaining the goal. This is basic human nature stuff. People can change. People can improve and innovate.

So now apply this to your organization. Can you think of anyone who hasn't attained their goal without deliberate effort? Do you know any organization that has improved accidently?

Does your organization have a short list of key goals (to honor the Pareto Principle: the vital few and trivial many)? Does your organization have disciplined and structured support to guide this change (Change Agent Skills delivered on an ongoing basis to your employees/ leaders responsible for influencing others)? Does your organization review feedback objectively in a regular basis to assess progress? Does your organization celebrate your wins on a regular basis? Are you changing and improving deliberately faster than your competitors? Are you satisfied with your process and results?

Successful Change Strategies - Why Bother?

So, only two things to do: improve and innovate.

Improvement targets the 10-30 percent of an organization's revenue being spent on generating waste. This waste is often hiding in their company processes. Employees and leaders must learn to see the waste, and then reduce/eliminate it. Lean and Six Sigma initiatives target some areas of companies.

Innovation targets new products and services to generate new revenue and profits. These opportunities are waiting to be unleashed from employee teams that have learned to promote and provoke new ideas.

Having the profits sooner to reinvest of course encourages us to improve and innovate - to change - sooner than later.

Successful Change Strategies - Mind the Heart

Considering the revenue and profit percentage points improving and innovating quickly adds to the bottom line, it's a wonder how some organizations can afford to spend so much time and resources on fire fighting.

Fire fighting is addictive. The busy-ness and activity surrounding fire fighting looks so much like work that many are led astray by a wide variety of new topic-of-the-month initiatives. "Hey, what are you guys working on - a, b, c or d?" "Well, all of them actually, isn't that what you're supposed to...?"

Only after the actual results of fire fighting are honestly evaluated does enough frustration occur to move company leaders to take the time and resources to build an internal company wide change capability. Improve and innovate, deliberately. That will keep you plenty busy and productive.

Successful Change Strategies - Assess Your Starting Point

All too often companies are pretty good at identifying ideas to improve and innovate but weak on the implementation, weak on the delivery. Good ideas get tackled by fear, pessimism, inertia, and politics. In my experience what is needed is a special team of employees/leaders who are responsible for moving the ideas through the implementation stages. Many call these people Change Agents. Good Change Agents help teams make better decisions that more team members support.

Is your organization staffed with capable Change Agents? Can your teams make and implement great decisions faster than your competitors?

What a wonderful opportunity - to not copy your competitors who will "save money" by not continuing to develop their change capability. One company hunkers down and weather's the storm. The other works through the rain and wind. Which company would you bet on when times get good again? It really depends on whether you see employee skills development as a cost or investment.

EXERCISE
Implementation Issues Report

Bring life to this topic by creating your own real list of promoting and restraining forces that will likely affect your change efforts. Work alone or with other participants.

I will suggest you complete this exercise with a flip chart sheet and some Post-Its. This will provide a large and flexible format to do your work.

1. Silently brainstorm write down descriptions of forces that will affect your change efforts; one idea per Post-It. Come up with 10 for each if you're working alone, or 5 per person if working with a team.

2. Meet with your table participants at the flip chart sheet. Divide the sheet into two columns: Promoting Forces, Restraining Forces

3. Presenting one idea at a time, move around your circle till everyone has discussed and posted all their ideas in the appropriate column. Do not pre-sort the Post-Its.

4. Once all the Post-Its are posted, silently organize the random Post-Its into groups of similar topics. Discuss to confirm the Post-Its are in the right spots and then title the groups.

5. Prioritize the groups of Post-Its by impact on your organization's success.

6. Discuss your findings; themes, principles, processes, etc.

You have created a list of forces to take advantage of (Promoting) and forces to consider and work to eliminate (Restraining). This list describes the playing field where you must win. Not completing this sort of exercise sends teams off on idealistic adventures hoping everything will be all right. It's unlikely that at the beginning everything is all right – that's why you have a yearning to change your organization.

Successful Change Attitudes – Considerations

A reminder: Do not dare to ask your employees to collaborate – to help build great decisions and great support, with lots of interactive, push-and-shove dialogue, and end with a team-supported decision unless you can. If you, at anytime, step to the side, and move to make a decision without any of the potential supporters' involvement, don't pretend that you want to collaborate.

In an example situation, the leader stays quiet during a series of meetings, listening to lots of dialogue but not contributing, hearing the team make and support a decision, claim the meeting a success, but return to their office and a few days letter, pronounce they have made a different decision to the betterment of the organization. The water coolers will be well staffed for weeks. The grapevine will record more hits than the company's website.

My view here is that these leaders are actually a constraint to the organization when they require making all the decisions that drive the company alone. In a growing organization, they will not have enough time to make enough good decisions to initiate the actions necessary to support the growth. Their need for control is a detriment to the organization. Alternatively the leader takes responsibility to build a culture that allows all employees to make appropriate decisions and drastically multiply the actions occurring to drive growth.

Short on Time?

You will at times not have the time you'd like to engage supporters in a full series of collaborative meetings. You may have to decide sooner. You still can though go to the supporters, explain the situation, and proactively answer any and all troublesome questions that you and some other leaders have thought of considering the likely reaction of the supporters. This at least provides the opportunity for you to inform and engage the supporters, still wanting and asking for their support, but working deliberately to anticipate and address any project-restraining ideas.

Senior Leaders: Listen Up

As I mentioned at the close of *Think or Sink,* seemingly off the radar screen, but likely the person with the most leverage to actually do something about this, is Bob Marchon, the executive VP of operations at the corporate office in Connecticut. If Bob Marchon learned and used collaborative approaches with his direct reports, they would become contagious. The way to do things around a company.

And although you may not have a position like Bob Marchon, if you are a leader, you can affect the people who report to you and are affected by the work you do.

Your Presentation

You do have some options as far as your approach as a change agent. One is to be the maniac on a mission. If your organization would allow you to be the louder champion, and keep your job, do so.

Alternatively, you may want to, and need to, be a little quieter in your approach. Joseph Juran can help here" "People do not dislike change, they dislike being changed." Chuck from *Think or Sink* shares the first letter of his name with Columbo, the detective from the TV series. Columbo is my facilitation hero. Quiet, deliberate, and always ready with the next good questions. I do not prefer, from *Think or Sink,* Louise (for the Lone Ranger) or Mark (for Mary Poppins)

Become an agent for change, noisy or quiet, whatever your audience will allow, and be the successful agent for change.

Pilot Teams

I am a real fan of pilot teams. If I want to develop an new skill set companywide (Six Sigma, Activity Based Costing, Improvement Teams, etc.) find four teams to work on real issues while learning the skills. If two or three of them "win," succeed in demonstrating the new skills does add value to your organization, the organization will welcome the subsequent company-wide introduction.

But if the organization goes company-wide from the start, (save the day, silver bullet, in on a white horse, etc), it is less likely you will succeed in having enough of the organization learn to like the change in the time your provide. You will then have to wait 6-12 months before the organization forgets the mess, and is ready for a new change.

For the pilot teams, provide a solid curriculum that helps the change agents build skills while working on real company issues.

Successful Change Agents – Considerations for Facilitators

A facilitator, by definition, is someone who helps others do their work. I will encourage anyone who knows how to use these tools to come to the aid of any team if the team will welcome it. So in any meeting, when the meeting gets stuck, someone can step forward and know which collaboration tool will be helpful.

To develop this expertise in an organization, to know which tool to use and how, one option is to have some employees trained formally. Alternatively, self driven individuals can learn from books like those in the Good Thinking Series, and have a positive effect in their organizations.

In the situation of important meetings, big decisions needing wide support, the leader of the initiative one ought to not facilitate. Their position or content might sway the meeting. Use a person from outside the group to do this.

10
Next Steps

So by now you should have enough to get started. Like approaching any change initiative you know that things will have to be different. If you're a change agent you likely want things to be different. The catch is this includes you —how you think, how you behave, how you get things done.

Find a willing team, practice your new skills boldly, and stay the course for 60-90 days, long enough to establish some new habits.

As we've read, our goal is to improve company performance by improving our thinking:

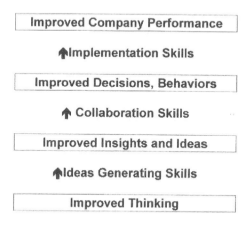

So your next steps will depend on your current situation. Here's a helpful series of questions:

- Select a business goal that needs attention.

- Identify the behaviors, decisions, and ideas that you would prefer to see.

- What thinking approach and style would produce the preferred ideas, behaviors and decisions that would deliver the business goal you seek?

- Then find a resource to help you learn to think that way.

The *Good Thinking Series* of books is an excellent way to learn to think more productively.

Good Thinking Series of Books - Overview

Good Thinking 1: Think or Sink: A Parable of Collaboration, introduces the Good Thinking approach to collaboration through a story of three leaders handling the same assignment.

Good Thinking 2: Collaborate (this book), introduces strategies and tools that can help you learn to work more collaboratively in a variety of situations with a variety of people and personalities.

Each of the four additional topics will provide a helpful process and supporting series of questions to accomplish tasks in those areas.

Good Thinking 3: Imagine will introduce techniques to generate ideas for today: process improvement (improve) and creative thinking skills (innovate).

Good Thinking 4: Plan will introduce techniques to generate ideas about tomorrow: strategic planning (improvement) and scenario planning (innovation).

As you likely know there are hundreds of resources to support leadership development. A quick trip to Google will send many suggestions your way.

The challenge here is to find resources that help you develop leaders that can differentiate your organization from your competitors. Everyone attending the same commercial training from the big guys will likely develop leaders that think more similarly. I encourage you to develop leadership training that helps your leaders think and behave in ways that best support your organization's goals, skills, and culture.

My *Good Thinking* curriculum provides onsite seminars and coaching that develop great collaborative leaders companywide by targeting leaders' thinking:

Idea Generating Skills

	Tactical	*Strategic*
Improve (Convergent)	Process Improvement Skills	Strategic Planning
	Collaboration Skills	
Innovate (Divergent)	Creative Thinking Skills	Scenario Planning

- **Process Improvement:** Learn to identify and replace sources of waste with value-added steps.

- **Creative Thinking Skills:** Learn to generate new ideas when you thought you couldn't think of any more.

- **Strategic Planning:** Create an operational planning document that guides company leaders and employees.

- **Scenario Planning:** Consider Alternative Futures: Think with your team about the future in a very productive way.

Implementing Skills

	Current Projects	New Projects
One Project	Project Management	Leading Change
Multiple Projects	Leading Teams	Leading an Innovative Organization

Collaboration Skills

- **Project Management:** Implement changes on an ongoing basis with teams who plan, manage, budget, track, and successfully complete company projects.

- **Leading Teams:** Initiate and support your organization's improvement teams.

- **Leading Change:** Learn and practice more effective ways to think about, and decide about, change and improvements.

- **Leading an Innovative Organization:** Help for senior leaders who are or will be leading an organization that embraces innovation.

Stamp Out Bad Bosses

Just one more stab at dysfunctional behavior. If you read through *Think or Sink,* you know how predictable, boring, and painful bad bosses are. You likely also know that people who leave companies most often are actually leaving their bosses.

A true story: my wife and I were sitting in our breakfast nook one morning, completing the cross word puzzle. With a minute to rest I pondered the day's *Dilbert* cartoon. In the first frame, Wally the Engineer told the Pointy-Haired Boss about a Swedish study that showed that people with bad bosses had forty percent more heart attacks. In the second frame, another worker sitting in the meeting seizes up and collapses with a heart attack. In the third frame, Wally says, "I should warn you that I'll probably tell this story a few more times."

I laughed for a while, wondering where does Scott Adams get his stuff..and bothered to go to the internet, and found:

Bad Boss? Your Heart May Feel the Heat - Los Angeles Times - November 25, 2008

"Anyone who's been in the job market long enough has sooner or later worked for a bad boss -- the kind, perhaps, who makes you start awake at 3 in the morning to fret about the day ahead or the horrible day that just happened.

"A new study suggests such bosses may increase the risk of a heart attack among employees, a finding that fits with other research on the effect of stress and . powerlessness on physical health. (See, for example, the famous Whitehall II study.)

"The latest study, published online today in the

journal Occupational and Environmental Medicine, tracked 3,122 working Swedish men ages 19 and 70 at the study's start. Their health was checked between 1992 and 1995 and their heart health outcomes tracked all the way up to 2003. At the start of the study the men were also asked to rate their managers' leaderships skills for such issues as -- per the paper -- "consideration for individual employees, provision of clarity in goals and role expectations, supplying information and feedback, ability to carry out changes at work successfully, and promotion of employee participation and control."

"During the period of time that was monitored, there had been 74 cases of ischemic heart disease (problems caused by narrow heart arteries, such as angina and heart attacks). Higher leadership scores were associated with a lower heart disease risk -- and the longer an employee worked at the same job with a good manager the lower his risk became. And vice versa.

"The researchers do note the possibility that the heart outcomes may have more to do with the personality of the people doing the rating -- after all, the bad-boss-good-boss perceptions were made by the employees themselves.

But, they write in their paper, "if the association is causal, this study suggests that interventions aimed at improving the psychosocial work environment and preventing ischemic heart disease among employees could focus on concrete managerial behaviors, such as the provision of clear work objectives, information and sufficient control in relation to responsibilities."

"Of course, one can think of other good reasons management might want to improve workforce leadership skills -- such as making a workplace more

pleasant (even if people aren't going to have heart attacks) and enhancing team performance."

—Rosie Mestel

So now I'm working on getting doctors to prescribe this book series...

Before that happens, I wish you good luck. Please contact me at *www.johncanfield.com* should you want to talk about the book, your boss, and your good results that have come from reading and implementing the ideas in *Collaborate* and the *Good Thinking Series* of books.

About the Author

John Canfield is an experienced business executive and coach who has been trained to facilitate a wide variety of planning, improvement, and innovation processes. John has many years of experience working and consulting in a wide variety of organizations around the world.

John has earned a B.S. in Mechanical & Industrial Engineering from the University of Minnesota and a B.A. in Political Science and Psychology from Williams College.

Prior to 1990 John was a Senior Engineering Manager for Intel Corporation and later Director of Corporate Quality and Design Research for Herman Miller.

To learn more about John please visit

Website: *www.johncanfield.com*

Article Series: *www.mibiz.com/goodthinking.html*

Videos: *www.youtube.com/canfieldgoodthinking*

LinkedIn: *www.linkedin.com/in/johncanfield*

• • •

Greg Smith is a writer, designer, and teacher. He collaborates on a variety of projects, in a wide-range of genres.

To learn more about Greg, please visit:

www.smithgreg.com

Made in the USA
Monee, IL
18 January 2020

20399533R00106